Your Daily Rock

A Daybook of Touchstones for Busy Lives

PATTI DIGH

Illustrated by Kim deBroin Mailhot

Lanha   *K*

For my rocks, always there, warm in the sunshine and reflective in the rain: John, Emma, and Tess Ptak. —Patti Digh

For David Mailhot. I always fly home to you. —Your Rock Fairy

TAYLOR TRADE PUBLISHING
An imprint of Rowman & Littlefield

Distributed by NATIONAL BOOK NETWORK

Copyright © 2014 by Patti Digh

Rock photographs by Keith Dixon of KeithDixonStudios.com

British Library Cataloguing-in-Publication Information available

Library of Congress Cataloging-in-Publication Data available

ISBN 978-1-4930-0652-6 (paperback)

∞™ The paper used in this publication meets the minimum requirements of American National Standard for Information Sciences—Permanence of Paper for Printed Library Materials, ANSI/NISO Z39.48-1992.

ON DAILY MINDFULNESS

We are enamored by projects that take place over time, aren't we? People who create a paper dress every day for a year, or who write a haiku every day for decades. We give gold watches to people who show up to their jobs for twenty-five years. There is a consistency in that practice over time that we admire.

What are our own daily practices? And how long do we sustain them before following again the path of least resistance, which is to stop? Mindfulness is a daily, incremental practice through which we build a foundation for our life.

How can we build a daily practice of mindfulness? There are many ways, and most involve a reminder of some sort—an "app" to remind us that mindfulness is ours for the having if we can take a moment to recenter. In this case, our app is a daily rock.

Why Rocks? Several years ago, I arrived at a reading I was doing in Deerfield, New Hampshire, to find a sparkly, dark-haired woman named Kim walking around with a basket of painted stones, inviting people to pick one at random. She turned to me, basket held out. I reached in, closed my eyes, and pulled out a stone that said "pain = change."

I knew in an instant I had received the right rock. The day before, a colleague had given me good, but painful, feedback. Pain = change, indeed. I turned to Kim and said, "You must be the Rock Fairy." And so she was.

Those rocks were powerful—not only to me, but to others. I bought them by the dozens to carry around the country and give out at book readings. Always, I asked people to close their eyes and pick one at random, and at every single reading, people came up to me, their eyes wide with the way the rock they had randomly chosen had big meaning in their lives.

How to Use This Book: This is designed as a daybook. I suggest you keep it on your bedside table. Each daily rock is brief enough to be read as you awaken. Read it, make note of the morning question, and come back to it as you go to bed to read and consider the evening question. You may find it rewarding to record your findings in the margins of this book or in a journal of your choosing.

With each rock, you'll find something to think about and/or do. Some will resonate with you, and some will not. Some will irritate you, and some will make you laugh. Some will be inconvenient, some will appear meaningless. And that's all okay. Every reaction you have is amazing and fantastic and right—for you. If the questions don't speak to your prism of experience, don't simply dismiss them—create your own. Ask yourself: What question will help me dive into this concept in a deeper way, relate it to my life?

You will learn much about how you approach life if you are mindful about how you approach this daily rock process. Where you find yourself uncomfortable, fantastic! That's an edge. And, truthfully, we only learn at our edges, not in our safe, comfy recliner. Pay attention to what you do at the edge. Most often we judge at our edges—we judge ourselves and we judge other people. Just notice what you notice at your edges—without judgment. When you come to an edge, you have to choose whether to judge or to learn, because you can't do both at the same time.

As novelist David Mitchell has written, "Travel far enough, you meet yourself." I hope these rocks serve as stepping-stones in that journey.

A time of new beginnings. Fresh starts. New com-
position notebooks. Sharpened pencils and cray-
ons. A time of vision boards and wishes, resolutions
and aspirations. Freedom from the year before. And
sometimes a period of great anxiety—can I live up to
my own expectations of myself? Is this going to be like
past years where I've done the things on my list for a
few weeks and then abandoned them? Are these things
I've said I want to achieve this year what is really in my
heart?

In journeying into a life of mindfulness, this incremental day-by-day process, you'll find January becoming less overwhelming and more the norm: Each day
will be a fresh start, a blank page, a moment to become
what you long to be (and what you already are).

January

We hear a lot about beginner's mind—the emptying out that allows us to really see and learn from a space of not-knowing. But I wonder if we let our striving-for-improvement mentality stand in the way of beginner's mind. Are we trying *too hard* to have beginner's mind? Can we reconcile both at the same time: moving forward *and* having a beginner's mind?

Saadat A. Khan suggests, "Beginner's mind embodies the highest emotional qualities such as enthusiasm, creativity, zeal, and optimism. If the reader reflects briefly on the opposites of these qualities, it is clear to see that quality of life requires living with beginner's mind. With beginner's mind, there is boundlessness, limitlessness, an infinite wealth."

Perhaps this year of Daily Rocks is, in fact, a journey into beginner's mind: Seeing what you have not seen before, days of boundless enthusiasm, creativity, zeal, and optimism.

Morning: Today, approach everything you do with a sense of optimism, even the most mundane of tasks or the most unfulfilling or difficult. Focus on feeling a lightness of being and thinking today.

Evening: In what ways did that spirit of optimism change your day?

January 1

"I've learned lately that no one is going to hand me a permission slip and tell me to take time out for me."

—WYNONNA JUDD

Today, give yourself permission to be cranky. Crank it up! Give yourself permission to screw up. Really mess it up in a big way! Give yourself permission to be less than perfect. You'll sleep better. You'll be happier. Give yourself permission to take time out for yourself. Then give yourself permission to love yourself even when you're cranky, even when you screw up, even when you are less than perfect, and even when you feel self-indulgent.

Morning: What will you give yourself permission to do today?

Evening: How did it feel to love all of yourself today, not just the nice, cheerful parts?

January 2

"Life is actually really simple, but we insist on making it complicated."

—CONFUCIUS

We are living in a culture of experts, some of whom believe their expert status is assured only if they make their wisdom complicated, so the rest of us will need to rely on them for the answer.

I don't think life is complicated at all—I think it is complex. And in a complexity no one has the answer for you. A complexity is not to be solved; it is to be walked into, embraced, danced with, not solved.

This calls on a whole different set of skills—not problem-solving, not drama-based, but internal and quiet and wise and still. The responses to complexities are simple wisdoms, small actions that focus on the quality of the relationship between you and the world, big knowings.

Morning: We are rewarded for problem-solving, but it is not the way into a complexity. It keeps us on the surface. Can you step away from problem-solving today? How might that look? Perhaps it means saying, "I don't know," instead of "I'll fix it."

Evening: How did it feel to sit with your innate, simple wisdom today instead of your problem-solving skills?

"I used to get caught up in drama, and now when there is drama, I just say 'wow.'"

—CINDY DOLLAR, YOGA TEACHER

In 2010, a friend of mine died in midsentence. Another died after two years with Lou Gehrig's disease. Another friend's life changed irrevocably in one regrettable instant. It was a year of loss. I told my friend Kurt. He sent back a one-line response: "Do you do yoga?" It was a perfect response. Yes, I needed to get out of my head and into my body.

I called a local yoga teacher and booked a private session. She knew I was there to mourn and to deepen my physical experience of loss, and she embraced that as she taught me simple poses.

We talked about loss and letting go. "I used to get caught up in drama," she said, "and now when there is drama, I just say 'wow.'" It is a form of detachment, that wow.

This simple wisdom has changed my life. Delta Airlines cancels my flight? A quiet wow. A friend betrays my confidence? Wow. Wow, with no attachment to outcome, without sarcasm or cynicism. Just wow. Detached from drama. A quiet, simple wow.

Morning: Can you say a quiet, simple "wow" today to detach from the drama that swirls around you?

Evening: How did it feel to approach drama in this way instead of being swept up into the drama itself?

January 4

"i carry your heart(i carry it in my heart)"

—E. E. CUMMINGS

When I traveled a lot (too much), Tess was young and bewildered, I know now, by my absences. The phrase we learned to say to each other was always this one: "I keep you in my heart." It reminds me of a favorite poem of mine by e. e. cummings, quoted above.

It also reminds me that space and time ultimately do not matter . . . though in the short term they often do, as in Tess's case. Even so, she (and I) were (and are) comforted by the image of ourselves in the other person's heart. (I can see that the sheer mention of e. e. cummings influences me to use parenthetical phrases willy-nilly.)

Morning: Who do you keep in your heart? Tell them today.

Evening: How did it feel to speak that love?

January 5

"Autopilot" is a cognitive state in which you act without self-awareness, a state in which you stay in the nest. Have you ever done that? Perhaps autopilot is something as simple as driving home from work and finding yourself at the last stoplight without realizing how you got there. Or waking up one morning to the realization that you've been sleepwalking through your life.

Let's turn off the autopilot today. Be fully here, completely awake. Fling yourself out of the nest.

Morning: Notice what you notice today about the ways in which you are on autopilot. Do you automatically reach for another cup of coffee? Do you take the same route to work every day? Are you steeling yourself against surprise?

Evening: How did it feel to notice those things today? In what ways can you "disrupt" that autopilot tomorrow?

January 6

"Creativity consists largely of rearranging what we know in order to find out what we do not know. To think creatively, we must be able to look afresh at what we normally take for granted."

—GEORGE KNELLER

As you go through this day, be mindful of what you take for granted. This is a big exercise in mindfulness, asking, "What else might be true?" at every juncture. That is beginning of creativity, of fresh thoughts, of aliveness.

For example, I take for granted that a cheese grater grates cheese. What else might I use it for? An earring holder, perhaps?

Morning: Today, pay attention to what you are taking for granted. Make a list of these thoughts.

Evening: What did you discover? Tomorrow, disrupt each of those things on your list by asking, "What else might be true?" What fresh thoughts can you have about each of those things?

January 7

We all need a little help sometimes. And often, we need help but
no one knows it. For many of us, it is so hard to ask for help.
Or, we may not have any idea what kind of help might be useful.

Today, how can you pay attention to what is both said and
unsaid in your life (by coworkers, family members, community
partners) and make a small gesture in their direction to say, "I
care"?

Morning: How can you be someone's angel in even a small way
today?

Evening: How did that attentiveness to others feel? In what way
were you someone's angel today?

January 8

"If you obsess over whether you are making the right decision,
you are basically assuming that the universe will reward you for
one thing and punish you for another. The universe has no fixed
agenda. Once you make any decision, it works around that decision.
There is no right or wrong, only a series of possibilities that shift
with each thought, feeling, and action that you experience."

—DEEPAK CHOPRA

You know that decision you've been considering? Being tentative has a place in our lives. It allows us to breathe, and think. And sometimes we need to commit. Today is that day. Commit or move on.

Morning: What decision will you finally make today?

Evening: How did it feel to make that decision?

January 9

*"When I say be creative, I don't mean you should all go
and become great painters and great poets. I simply mean
let your life be a painting, let your life be a poem."*

—OSHO

We so segregate art from life, as if they are two separate things.
What if we reconnected them, and saw our everyday life as a
work of art? How would that change how we see our days?
Would that allow us to see the beauty in the ordinary?

There is poetry in every moment, every gesture, every
glance, every hesitation, and every leap.

Morning: How can you let your life be a poem today? Or a
painting?

Evening: What artfulness did you find in your day today?

January 10

"If you insist on disavowing that which is ugly about what you do, you will never learn from your mistakes."

—CASSANDRA CLARE

I know we all make mistakes in our lives. We all hurt others, intentionally or unintentionally. I don't mind that—I think that is how we learn and move forward. But we can't learn and move forward if we don't own those mistakes, if we explain them as merely someone else's "story" about us, someone else's "interpretation" of our actions. Let us own our actions, learn from them, tell the truth about them, and embrace them, not "spin" them.

Morning: What do you need to own about yourself today in order to learn from it?

Evening: What did you own about yourself today? In what ways did you do that? How did that feel?

January 11

"What should young people do with their lives today? Many things, obviously. But the most daring thing is to create stable communities in which the terrible disease of loneliness can be cured."

—KURT VONNEGUT

We are tribal creatures, at our best in moments of healthy community and connection—those structures of belonging that can buoy and sustain us. Creating our "tribe" sometimes means rejecting tribes that aren't healthy for us, that don't encourage us but bring us down or make us small. Seek out people who challenge and support you instead.

Morning: What one step can you take toward either creating or strengthening your tribe today?

Evening: What does finding your own tribe mean to you? What step did you take today?

*"Neatness, madam, has nothing to do with the truth.
The truth is quite messy, like a windblown room."*

—WILLIAM J. HARRIS

One afternoon last year, I picked Tess up from school and her pants were covered in dirt. Her teacher walked over to me and apologized that Tess was so dirty, explaining their time on the playground that day. "No apology necessary!" I said. "This is truly the mark of a fabulous day!"

Do you ever allow yourself to get messy? Do you ever walk in the rain, or do you worry about getting your clothes wet? Do you tell kids not to get dirty? What would happen if you didn't? Life is messy—let's embrace that mess!

Morning: Today, get messy.

Evening: How did that feel? What childhood messages did you have to overcome to do that?

January 13

"Now this is very profound, what rhythm is, and goes far deeper than words. A sight, an emotion, creates this wave in the mind, long before it makes words to fit it . . ."

—VIRGINIA WOOLF

Our lives have rhythms to them, but because we are addicted to words, we can't feel them. What we see and touch and feel, as Virginia Woolf says, creates waves in our minds—beyond words, deeper than words. Sometimes our own heartbeat is a rhythm we can't hear.

Our refrigerators have a rhythm. The wind. Our legs when we walk. The sky and clouds. Emotions. There is rhythm all around us. We experience so little of it.

Morning: Can you let yourself ride that wave of rhythm without reducing it to words?

Evening: Did you dance to the rhythm of your life today?

January 14

"Sleep is the best meditation."

—DALAI LAMA

I'm with the Dalai Lama on this one. Curl up for a nice nap as soon as you can. The world needs more well-rested, meditative, peaceful energy in it. Put clean sheets on your bed and enjoy the coolness of them.

Morning: Can you allow yourself the precious luxury of a nap one day soon? How about today?

Evening: Do you get enough sleep? Do you ever feel well rested? What excuses do you give yourself for being sleep-deprived?

January 15

meet someone new.

When my friend Nina was dying, I spent her last weekend at the rest home, keeping her company. A friend of hers came to visit and I took the opportunity to walk down the hall toward the dining room. One of the workers I had befriended called to me, "C'mon in for dinner."

When I got my food, and was trying to figure out the seating arrangements, she told me to go sit with Harry.

"Who?"

"Harry," she said. "He's right there at the first table." Harry was slumped over in his chair, and my first thought was, "I can't do this. I haven't eaten, I haven't slept for days, my friend is dying, and I don't even know if this slumped-over man can communicate." But sit I did, and Harry and I became quick friends, then and now.

Morning: What opportunities do you have to connect with another human being? How often do you have my initial reaction, that meeting someone new is too hard, too tiring, too much?

Evening: What might happen if you extended yourself in those situations instead?

January 16

"I was going to die, sooner or later, whether or not I had even spoken myself. My silences had not protected me. Your silences will not protect you. What are the words you do not yet have? What are the tyrannies you swallow day by day and attempt to make your own, until you will sicken and die of them, still in silence?"

—AUDRE LORDE

I am going to let the words of the powerful Audre Lorde continue to lead us in speaking up:

> Once you start to speak, people will yell at you. They will interrupt you, put you down and suggest it's personal. And the world won't end. And the speaking will get easier and easier. And you will lose some friends and lovers, and realize you don't miss them. And new ones will find you and cherish you. And at last you'll know with surpassing certainty that only one thing is more frightening than speaking your truth. And that is not speaking.

Speak it, Audre. Speak it.

Morning: Practice speaking up today. Let Audre Lorde be your inspiration.

Evening: What words do you not yet have? How will you get them?

January 17

"*I prefer to explore the most intimate moments, the smaller,
crystallized details we all hinge our lives on.*"

—RITA DOVE

We think of explorers as bold men and women going where no one has gone before. We think of great expeditions, Sherpas, grand expanses. We think of big moments, like a huge Chicago musical, in which big things get played out. And yet, our lives hinge on those smaller, crystallized details poet Rita Dove explores. Throw a hula hoop on your back lawn, or a circle of string on your bedside table, or a rubber band on your desk and watch inside that space for a week, that tiny space. Explore that small circle. Be a tiny explorer. That's where the living is.

Morning: What small frame will you create in which to start exploring today?

Evening: What did you notice in that frame today?

January 18

"We are all wonderful, beautiful wrecks. That's what connects us—that we're all broken, all beautifully imperfect."

—EMILIO ESTEVEZ

We are all wonderful, beautiful wrecks. And yet we try so hard to hide the cracks. What if we displayed them instead? Like the Japanese who fix broken pottery with seams of gold. *Kintsugi*, this process is called: "It makes no attempt to hide the crack, but incorporates it as a design element into something simultaneously broken and strengthened by the break."

Morning: Into what beautiful cracks can you pour gold?

Evening: Imagine your life as a piece of pottery. Now imagine all those veins of gold adorning it. Trace each one with your finger and thank it for the beauty and realness it has brought to your vessel.

January 19

*"Tender," she said again. "Tender is kind and gentle.
It's also sore, like the skin around an injury."*

—BRENNA YOVANOFF

I love that quote about what it is to be tender. We often think of "tender" as kind and gentle; not so often as skin healing after a wound. Both are tender, and both are important. My ring finger on my left hand is numb at the very tip from learning to play the fiddle, pressing so intently on the string with it. I find myself aware of that numb soreness, more than I am aware of my other fingertips. Sometimes tenderness is a way of focusing, the soreness a way of grounding our attention in the moment. Be fully tender today; focus on what is sore.

Morning: What tender spots do you have? How can you focus on them today?

Evening: What did you learn from focusing on those tender spots today?

"I don't like that man. I must get to know him better."

—ABRAHAM LINCOLN

There are so many things we don't know. Is it possible to walk toward those things with a curiosity rather than a condemnation? Is it possible to walk toward them with a sense of wonder rather than fleeing in the opposite direction? I've found this phrase to be the best way to explore with curiosity: "Help me understand . . ." Not "how could you?" or "why do you?" or "why don't you?" but "help me understand."

It opens up a dialogue rather than shutting it down. Help me understand the significance of your wearing a turban, kilt, cross, other article of clothing. What does that mean to you? Help me understand your beliefs about marriage equality, about end-of-life issues, about . . . Help me understand. So much of the time we avoid difference or judge it rather than explore it because we've confused noticing difference with making a judgment. What if we could be respectfully childlike instead: Help me understand. Start a conversation with "Help me understand . . ." today.

Morning: Use "Help me understand" at least three times today in your interactions with others. Notice what happens.

Evening: What did you discover?

"My religion is very simple. My religion is kindness."

—DALAI LAMA

A few years ago, as part of a live radio interview, a journalist asked me what I wanted to have written on my tombstone. I answered without hesitation, though I hadn't thought of it before: "She was kind and she was generous." To me, kindness is holy. And it is generous. Both are heart-focused, and if I had to describe an action that might represent them both, it would be of a heart opening up—to ourselves, and to others. Because in order to be truly and authentically kind and generous to others, we must first extend that grace to ourselves. That, in fact, might be the harder to do. Why do we imagine kindness is only directed outward, and not inward as well?

Morning: What is your answer to that journalist's question? Are you living in a way that will inspire those words to be engraved on that tombstone after you are gone? If not, what needs to change?

Evening: In what ways were you kind and generous today?

January 22

"Blessed are the hearts that can bend; they shall never be broken."

—ALBERT CAMUS

In June 1992, I was hugely pregnant with my older daughter, Emma, and at a conference in Las Vegas. At 4:57 a.m. on June 28th, I woke up to what I knew immediately was an earthquake, though I had never experienced one before. The building rolled and tilted; I watched as my clothes swayed back and forth in the closet of my room on the nineteenth floor, and as the water sloshed out of the toilet bowl with each lurch.

In that moment, I understood what it means to bend, to move *with* instead of against. All that bendiness saved a lot of lives that day.

Morning: How can your heart become "bendier" today? Notice where you are static and where you are bendy today.

Evening: Is your life bendy? In what ways could you make it bendier?

January 23

"Home wasn't a set house, or a single town on a map. It was wherever the people who loved you were, whenever you were together. Not a place, but a moment, and then another, building on each other like bricks to create a solid shelter that you take with you for your entire life, wherever you might go."

—SARAH DESSEN

Every time I travel, my Facebook update on the morning when I wake up, pack, and get ready to come home is always this: "Let's fly away home." There is a sense of great satisfaction when I can say those words—as much as I adore the people I meet when I travel, there comes a time to relax and set down my luggage. I know "home" may not be that place for everyone, but each of us needs someplace we can fly away to, that place that gives us comfort. Perhaps that is home, and perhaps it is somewhere else, somewhere closer. As Buddha said, "Do not look for a sanctuary in anyone except yourself."

Morning: Where is "home" for you? Can you find it inside yourself today?

Evening: How can you cultivate your own Self as your sanctuary over the coming weeks?

January 24

"The primary sign of a well-ordered mind is a man's ability to remain in one place and linger in his own company."

—SENECA

Morning is a time to linger longer, one hand on the handle of your mug, one on the *New York Times*. Evening is a time to linger longer, standing in the kitchen for a moment after cooking dinner, just smelling the spices. Night is a time to linger longer, after putting your children to bed, standing at the door watching them sleep. Sunshine is a time to linger longer, standing outside for an extra minute before going into work, your face toward the sky. A lake is a time to linger longer, sitting on the shore, looking at the trees on the other bank, silently. Linger just a little longer today.

Morning: What needs to happen in your daily schedule to allow for lingering longer?

Evening: How did it feel to linger just a bit more today, to savor?

January 25

"I believe we learn by practice. Whether it means to learn to dance by practicing dancing or to learn to live by practicing living, the principles are the same. In each, it is the performance of a dedicated precise set of acts, physical or intellectual, from which comes shape of achievement, a sense of one's being, a satisfaction of spirit. . . . Practice means to perform, over and over again in the face of all obstacles, some act of vision, of faith, of desire. Practice is a means of inviting the perfection desired."

—MARTHA GRAHAM

I love this word, "practice." Sure, I practice my fiddle. And I practiced piano for fifteen years' worth of lessons before then. And I'm practicing saying "no" to sugar. In addition to those external, physical practices, I want to practice some internal stuff too.

I want to practice: Noticing my first thought (which might look like a knee-jerk reaction) and working on my second (which looks a lot like empathy and love and understanding). Pausing for twenty-four hours before responding to an invitation to give myself time to feel the answer. Asking myself "What would love do?" in times of great irritation and in times of great peace. Remembering to extend grace to myself when I screw up.

Morning: What would you like to invite into your life by creating a practice?

Evening: How can you remind yourself to practice this every day?

January 26

"It does not matter how slowly you go as long as you do not stop."

—CONFUCIUS

One of my favorite short-story writers is Ron Carlson. He also wrote a book about the writing of one of his short stories, walking the reader through the whole process. It's called *Ron Carlson Writes a Story*. In it, among other things, he says the writer is the person who stays in the room: "The most important thing a writer can do after completing a sentence is to stay in the room. The great temptation is to leave the room to celebrate the completion of the sentence or go out in the den where the television lies like a dormant monster and rest up for a few days for the next sentence or to go wander the seductive possibilities of the kitchen."

This is advice not just for writers. In my fiddle classes, I have noticed my almost irrepressible desire to celebrate a conquered musical phrase, sometimes to the bewilderment of my teacher when I stop mid-song to do so. I get it right, and then lose concentration, unable to continue. And in that recognition, I can see other parts of my life, those times when I leave the room to celebrate rather than stay the course. I'm all for celebration. And for recognizing when I need to stay in the room.

Morning: How can you stay in the room today?

Evening: How can you stay in the room tomorrow?

January 27

"Forgiveness does not change the past, but it does enlarge the future."

—PAUL BOESE

I recently felt betrayed by someone very close to me. Lies were told. Secrets were created where none had been before. And so much more. My first reaction? I got angry. But not at him (oh, that would come later). I got angry at myself: "How could you have been so stupid? How could you have trusted him? How could you not have seen this coming? How could you have been so fooled for so long?"

We do this, don't we? In the face of irrefutable evidence that the person lying to us is a sociopath, or worse, we question ourselves. We blame ourselves for being too trusting, too naive, too blind to the mounting evidence. We get angry at ourselves. That anger will eat you up from the inside out.

I finally had to say this out loud to myself: "Patti, I forgive you for not knowing. I forgive you your anger toward yourself. I forgive you for eating too much in times of stress. I forgive you for the disappointment you are still holding onto. You deserve a larger future."

Morning: What do you want or need to forgive yourself for? Say it out loud. Let it go.

Evening: In what ways do you betray yourself?

January 28

*"Every child is an artist. The problem is how to
remain an artist once he grows up."*

—PABLO PICASSO

Art changes lives. It even saves lives. We know this. Aristotle has
said that "the aim of art is to represent not the outward appear-
ance of things, but their inward significance." That's how art
saves us—it's not the form of the art, but the process of it. And
yet we deflect our creative spirits in so many ways: "I'm not an
artist." "I don't have an artistic bone in my body." "I'm not creative." What if we stopped doing that?

We can tell a different story. What if we stepped into our
creative spirits fully, the ones we had when we were four years
old? That's the real us, before we started comparing ourselves
to other people, before we started expecting too much of ourselves, before we fully invested in the story of "not enough."
What if "make art" could mean whatever we wanted it to? What
if our life's meaning could only be revealed by the external rep-
resentation of what's inside of us?

Morning: What art will you make today?

Evening: How did it feel to make art today? What did you learn
in the process?

January 29

"Walk as if you are kissing the Earth with your feet."

—THÍCH NHẤT HẠNH

I am not always joyful. Are you? In fact, I am often overcome by the bigness of the sadness and inequity in the world. Sometimes I am in great pain, for myself or others. Life sometimes feels big and panicked and hurtful. And even in those moments, I know I have a choice: I can make a choice that closes me down, or I can make a choice that opens me up. I can choose, as William Wordsworth suggested, to live with an eye made quiet by the power of harmony, and the deep power of joy, so I can see into the life of things. That is always a choice we can make. Choose the deep power of joy today.

Morning: How can I remind myself today to choose joy even when things go "wrong"?

Evening: What joy did you find in this day?

"Your problem is how you are going to spend this one odd and precious life you have been issued. Whether you're going to spend it trying to look good and creating the illusion that you have power over people and circumstances, or whether you are going to taste it, enjoy it and find out the truth about who you are."

—ANNE LAMOTT

Let's do that second part: Taste it, enjoy it and find out the truth about who you are.

Every day. Because tomorrow isn't guaranteed.

Morning: How will you give up looking good today in order to taste life?

Evening: How did it feel to let go of play-acting today and just be you?

This month, focus on consistency. You've started, now continue. Make mindfulness a daily practice, one you leap into rather than dread. Or one you wake into. A way into a richer, more creative life rather than another "to do" item on your list, something that weighs you down.

Read, reflect, practice, reflect. That is the rhythm of these days. Dive into February with renewed passion for living a life full of laughter, love, and meaning.

February

"Grasping at things can only yield one of two results: Either the thing you are grasping at disappears, or you yourself disappear. It is only a matter of which occurs first."

—GOENKA

Every confrontation or dispute arises from two or more people each demanding they are right. And it is this clinging to being right that causes us the most pain, not the situation itself.

Ask yourself these four questions when you are stubbornly clinging to being right:

- Why do you think you are so attached to being right about this situation? (Note: Because you *are* right is not a valid answer, no matter how much we'd love for it to be.)
- Why is being right about this so important to you?
- Doesn't everyone have their own version of "right"?
- I wonder what would happen if you gave up your need to be right?

Morning: Notice today when you are pushing on the "I'm right" button. Notice what it feels like to let that go, to give up your need to be right (even if you are right).

Evening: As you end this day, let go of what you were "right" about today.

February 1

"As if you were on fire from within. The moon
lives in the lining of your skin."

—PABLO NERUDA

What makes you shine from the inside out?
    Spend more time near that fire.

Morning: Imagine today that the moon is living in the lining of
your skin. Focus on letting that light shine through your pores.

Evening: How did it feel to shine today?

February 2

"The question is not what you look at, but what you see."

—HENRY DAVID THOREAU

We see very little of the world around us. We are rushing so quickly to arrive somewhere: At work, at peace, at the weight we want to be.

In this world of ours, there is room for amazement. There is room for focus, for seeing beyond the blur at 70 mph. In this life of yours, there is room to see what you want to see—so start looking for what you want your life to be, not what you don't want it to be.

Morning: Today, see the color orange. See generosity. See the color of the sky. See the beauty of scars. See fulfillment.

Evening: What did you notice in focusing your sight on specific things today?

February 3

*"We sleep, but the loom of life never stops, and the
pattern which was weaving when the sun went down
is weaving when it comes up in the morning."*

—HENRY WARD BEECHER

I love libraries for many reasons, among them this one: Wandering in library stacks is a beautifully physical way to follow a thread as you pick up a book and notice the one next to it, and another in the next row that stands out for whatever reason. And suddenly a whole tapestry of knowing, and understanding, has been woven by those threads—if we don't stop the process by "staying on task."

Morning: What thread can you allow yourself to follow today?

Evening: What did you discover in following that thread today?

February 4

"*I don't want to live in the kind of world where we don't look out for each other. Not just the people that are close to us, but anybody who needs a helping hand. I can't change the way anybody else thinks, or what they choose to do, but I can do my bit.*"

—CHARLES DE LINT

Sometimes helping others is not convenient. You have other plans. You have a full plate. You need help yourself.

That's when it is important.

That's when it matters.

That's when it counts.

Morning: How can you help someone today?

Evening: What did you do today to help someone else? How did that feel?

February 5

"To pay attention, this is our endless and proper work."

—MARY OLIVER

We are so distracted. Texting while eating. Checking e-mail while talking. Taking phone calls while driving.

The list goes on. What does fully paying attention even look like anymore?

When someone talks to you on the phone, are you surreptitiously checking Facebook? When a child asks for your attention, do you keep typing? When your partner asks if you can sit and talk, do you beg off until later?

Morning: As a start, can you put down your electronics today?

Evening: Tomorrow, can you do only one thing at a time? If you are drinking coffee, only drink coffee. If you are walking, only walk. If you are talking to someone, turn and face them completely.

February 6

"Look within. Within is the fountain of good, and it will ever bubble up, if thou wilt ever dig."

—MARCUS AURELIUS

Sitting quietly with ourselves is something we too often forget to do. Why is that? Is it because we are afraid of what we might find in that silence? What might we find if we dig not into the stockpiles of answers outside ourselves, but within, instead? Might we discover the wellsprings of that fountain of good?

Morning: Today, how can you dig within to free the goodness and wisdom you possess?

Evening: Did you trust yourself today? That internal knowing—did you fully respect it today?

February 7

"Happiness is excitement that has found a settling down place. But there is always a little corner that keeps flapping around."

—E. L. KONIGSBURG

That little corner that keeps flapping around? That's where the glee is. But aren't those the corners we try to tie, stitch into conformity, duct-tape down?

We look for glee in the big moments of our lives, but it is really in those tiny ones at the edges. You're in charge of grabbing the corner and flapping it today. Carry on, Glee Warrior.

Morning: Look for the moments of corner flapping today. They are there. Let it fly.

Evening: How does glee feel to you? How can you let more corners of glee into your life on a daily basis?

February 8

"Because philosophy arises from awe, a philosopher is bound in his way to be a lover of myths and poetic fables. Poets and philosophers are alike in being big with wonder."

—THOMAS AQUINAS

Children are our greatest teachers in awe—they are so big with wonder.

"IT'S SNOWING!"

"LOOK AT THIS FLOWER!"

"I CAN HEAR MY HEART BEAT!"

"WHEN YOU HUG ME, I FEEL LIKE CHOCOLATE!"

Morning: Be awed by the sky today. Or the snow. Or electricity. Or the way your heart keeps beating. Or the feeling of a hug.

Evening: What awed you today? If nothing, what kept you from awe?

February 9

"Three things in human life are important: the first is to be kind; the second is to be kind; and the third is to be kind."

—HENRY JAMES

I have realized it is easy to be kind to people who are kind to us, isn't it? That's not where the heart of kindness lives. It lives in being kind to people who are hateful to you, in asking, "What is the kindest response I can offer?"

Morning: Today, be kind, even (and especially) in the face of unkindnesses toward you. That is all. And that is enough.

Evening: What kindness challenges did you face today? How did you resolve them?

February 10

"Anyone who has never made a mistake has never tried anything new."

—ALBERT EINSTEIN

It's no wonder we have such a hard time letting ourselves make mistakes. We grow up in a world in which mistakes = bad. Big red marks on our school papers, demotions, things that fall apart and can't be put back together in the same way. And we don't keep those things outside of ourselves, do we? No, we internalize these messages of "wrong" into ourselves, so suddenly *we* are the mistake.

The paralysis that comes with avoiding mistakes also leads us to avoid creativity, innovation, movement forward. And "mistakes" don't have anything to do with our core self—they don't define who we are as people.

Morning: Try something new today. Make mistakes. Celebrate them.

Evening: How does it feel to celebrate mistakes rather than hide them or run away from them?

February 11

"As we work to create light for others, we naturally light our own way."

—MARY ANNE RADMACHER

When we give freely, we become fully human, lit up from the inside out. It is an act of expansiveness, a generative process of letting go of measuring or being attached to the outcome. We can feel ourselves expand in the process of giving freely.

Not so when we give in anticipation of receiving, when there is thought of "if I give, then I expect to receive." That is a closing down, a tightening, a demand for reciprocity that requires no generosity, just expectation.

Light yourself up by creating light for others. Be a lightning bug for kindness and generosity.

Morning: Give something away today—something you love, time you think you can't spare, a note of gratitude to someone.

Evening: How might you freely give tomorrow?

"May your life preach more loudly than your lips."

—WILLIAM ELLERY CHANNING

Perhaps we all sound better on paper. It is hard to walk what we talk every day—because if we're doing it well, it's a constant practice. So the walking and the talking are all works-in-progress on the best of days. And that's okay. Because we know when there's a gap between what we talk and what we walk. Our gut knows it. And so do the people around us. Our job is to mind that gap every day and make the distance between the walk and the talk as narrow as possible, a gap we can reach across at all times, allowing us to sample from both sides, one informing the other.

Because we never get there, but straddle that gap all our lives. And that's a beautiful journey.

Morning: What are four values by which you say you want to live your life? After you write those down, pay attention today to how they show up (or don't) in your life.

Evening: What gaps did you straddle today?

"The strongest love is the love that can demonstrate its fragility."

—PAULO COELHO

When in doubt, love. With your whole heart. Not only if you are loved in that way, but also if you are not. That is all you need to know; that is all you need to do.

Love that is always strong and true and reciprocated is false, but we can only love fully if we can own the truth that loving comes with breaking, that opening our heart fully means we can allow it to shatter, or be ignored or rejected. And in the face of all evidence to the contrary, can open our hearts fully anyway.

Morning: Exude love today. Not just for your closest loves, but for the whole world. The whole world, even those bits you believe to be unlovable.

Evening: What does the word "fragile" mean to you?

February 14

Contribute.

"Do more than belong: participate. Do more than care: help.
Do more than believe: practice. Do more than be fair: be kind.
Do more than forgive: forget. Do more than dream: work."

—WILLIAM ARTHUR WARD

We can't do everything, but we can do something.

How can you make the world better today? Think small. Think ripples.

Participate, help, practice, be kind, forget, work. Which of these calls to you as a way to contribute? Life is a verb: Choose one.

Morning: If there is something that needs doing today, find a way to do it. Engage, step up, make the contribution that only you can make.

Evening: Action feels good, doesn't it? What can you contribute tomorrow?

February 15

"Piglet noticed that even though he had a Very Small Heart, it could hold a rather large amount of Gratitude."

—A. A. MILNE

In fact, gratitude enlarges your heart. (In a good way, not in that get-thee-to-the-ER-immediately kind of way.) It opens up space in you for love, for happiness, for contentment. It opens up space in you for life.

Morning: Say thank you ten times today.

Evening: Before you go to bed tonight, list at least five things you were grateful for today. If you can continue this each night, soon you will find that this practice reframes your days into expeditions as you search for things to feel gratitude for—and this will change your life's focus.

February 16

"In today's world, no one gets lost anymore. We pull up a GPS on our cell phones, type in our destination, and get step-by-step directions to where we want to go. Many of us also have a mental map, a personal GPS, telling us where we want to go in our life. It's great to have an idea of where we want to go in our life. It's great to have an idea of how to get there, but you can gain even more when you veer off your map."

—RABBI JULIE WOLKOFF

My friend Jodi Cohen once told me about a friend who stood at the edge of the Grand Canyon, fiddling with his GPS, saying, "I don't know where we are."

"We're right here," she told him. "We're right here."

Morning: Magic can happen when we get lost. Turn off your GPS. Let yourself be right here today.

Evening: How can you get lost tomorrow?

February 17

"Mindfulness meditation doesn't change life. Life remains as fragile and unpredictable as ever. Meditation changes the heart's capacity to accept life as it is."

—SYLVIA BOORSTEIN

Awareness and mindfulness are two different things.

Mindfulness is awareness pointed in a certain direction, on purpose, and (this is important) without judgment.

Mindfulness helps us recognize our way out of patterns that no longer serve us, without judging ourselves for having created those patterns in the first place. Judgment, on the other hand, kicks us right out of learning.

Morning: Pay attention on purpose today, in each moment, without judgment.

Evening: What patterns did you discern today? If there were negative ones, can you let go of judging yourself for them?

February 18

"We are the yearning creatures of this planet."

—ROBERT OLEN BUTLER

Writer Robert Olen Butler explains that the plot of any story is a yearning meeting a series of obstacles. The story doesn't move forward without that desire—or without those obstacles.

So let yourself yearn, that deepest form of desire, and let yourself embrace the obstacles that move your story forward. Don't live so much in your head that you lose track of yearning, and don't run from the obstacles, but let them be your teacher instead.

Morning: What do you yearn for? Let yourself long for that today. Notice what you believe stands in your way to getting to that destination.

Evening: How can those obstacles be your best teacher?

February 19

"Optimism is a strategy for making a better future. Because unless you believe that the future can be better, you are unlikely to step up and take responsibility for making it so."

—NOAM CHOMSKY

We must see ourselves in the stories of need we see on the nightly news. What keeps us from doing that? What makes it possible to disassociate so radically that we do not demand the changes that must occur for people to live and die in dignity, not in squalor, in fear, in hopelessness?

We must consider ourselves part of the solution in order for any change to occur. We must be optimistic in order to do that. Instead of asking, "Why aren't *they* doing more?" I must ask, "Why aren't *we* doing more?" and, finally, "Why am *I* not doing more?"

Morning: Put out your antenna for each time you think, "They really should do something about that." How can you consider yourself part of the solution instead?

Evening: What keeps you from exercising your optimism as a strategy for making a better future?

"Blessings don't come as luck. They are our daily dose. For a mere fact that we can blink, chew, frown, and smile means we are blessed. Waking up in the morning is a blessing that we should always give thanks to."

—PABALLO SEIPEI

Sometimes life is so dark that if someone suggests we are blessed, we fight back, we deny, we participate fully in the oppression Olympics, focusing on what is wrong so they will understand our pain. That is a purely human reaction; we all do it sometimes.

And yet.

Just on the other side of any darkness is our shared understanding that taking even one more breath is a blessing. Our job is to remember that.

Morning: Today, let "This day is a blessing" be your mantra. Repeat it as often as you can during the day.

Evening: How did that change things? How did it feel?

February 21

"If you listen carefully, you can hear these things. If you look carefully, you'll see what you're after."

—HARUKI MURAKAMI

Today, see. Take a long look.

Morning: Find five minutes today to sit and look at the world around you.

Evening: Can you incorporate five minutes in your day tomorrow (and beyond) to simply sit with the world to take a long look?

"I find hope in the darkest of days, and focus in the brightest. I do not judge the universe."

—DALAI LAMA

Some things I know for sure: 1) We do not always choose our circumstances. But we always choose how we are in those circumstances. 2) We see what we expect to see. 3) We judge the universe a lot.

How are you in your circumstance? How else might you be in it?

What do you expect to see?

What would giving up judging the universe look and feel like?

Morning: Take those questions with you as you enter your day today.

Evening: What did you learn? Do you focus on the good? If not, how can you?

February 23

"*I want you to use your voice. . . . I want you to be loud and fierce
and wild, unable to be tamed. . . . I want to know that every bit of
power you were born with has been harnessed and is in full use so that
when you need strength, you won't have to rely on your reserves. . . .
You will meet people who will want you to shrink back so that they
can step into the spotlight and claim all the warmth. Don't let them.
Move forward, take the light, accept the applause, understand how
brilliant you are. People will inevitably say mean things to you or about
you; don't suck those things under your skin and try to make sense
of them. Bust forth, make demands, speak up, don't shy down.*"

—CHI SHERMAN, IN *WHAT I WISH FOR YOU: SIMPLE WISDOM FOR A HAPPY LIFE*

Roar, baby. Roar.

Morning: How does being fierce look for you? It looks different
for all of us. Be fierce in your beautiful, individual way today.

Evening: Tomorrow, focus on this part of being fierce: "Don't
shy down." Even introverts know they can bust forth in a way
that feels good for them. Do that.

February 24

"It takes a lot of courage to show your dreams to someone else."

—ERMA BOMBECK

Why are we reticent to show our dreams to others? Because they might shoot down the idea, or tell us we're not ready, or that it's been done before, or that we're not special, or it will cost too much, or we're taking on too much. The list of "no" to dreams is almost endless. But "no" is just a tiny two-letter word, hardly big enough to count as a real word.

The only one who needs to believe in your dream is you. Sharing it is a way of showing that you believe in it. Let the response be what it may—your job is to make the strong offer.

Morning: Today, own your bravery. Share your dreams.

Evening: How does it feel to be brave?

February 25

"There comes a day when you realize turning the page is the best feeling in the world, because you realize there's so much more to the book than the page you were stuck on."

—ZAYN MALIK

Read the whole book of your life. You can't do that until you go past the page you're on. Unstick. Turn the page.

Morning: What page are you stuck on? Who are the characters on that page? What is the plot at this part of the story? If today were a scene in the book of your life, how would it be written?

Evening: Write that scene. Then turn the page. What scene do you want to write tomorrow?

February 26

*"Remember there's no such thing as a small act of kindness.
Every act creates a ripple with no logical end."*

—SCOTT ADAMS

Our job is to start those ripples; we cannot control where they go. Ripples can't ripple if we hold on to them.

Start a kindness ripple today, and let it go where it will.

Morning: What "small" act of kindness will you do today?

Evening: What "small" act of kindness will you do tomorrow? What if this were a daily practice for you?

February 27

"Human freedom involves our capacity to pause between the stimulus and the response and, in that pause, to choose the one response toward which we wish to throw our weight. The capacity to create ourselves, based upon this freedom, is inseparable from consciousness or self-awareness."

—ROLLO MAY

We treat pauses as necessary evils. What if they are necessary angels instead?

Pauses help us catch our breath. They allow us to move from reacting to responding, from action to reflection and then back to action again. They let us see things from a still point outside the fray. They give us perspective and a chance to notice our first thought, and work on our second.

Hurry, hurry, pause. Hurry, hurry, pause. Let this be the rhythm of your life until it can be Pause, hurry, pause. Pause.

Morning: Take note of how often you allow yourself to pause today.

Evening: Many of us are raised in a culture of "put your hand up first in school to show how smart you are," so pausing may need to be relearned. Practice.

February 28

My thoughts exactly.

Leap year calls for leaping. One year I celebrated by taking a trapeze lesson. What can you do to celebrate your leap year?

Morning: How will you leap today?

Evening: Why don't you leap more often?

February 29

When the wind blows it brings a chill, sometimes, and fresh air. Just enough to invigorate us, to give us a promise of the months to come, to hold us to our word.

When we are rushing through life, we sometimes think speeding up is the only way through. In reality, our most potent action is sometimes the counterintuitive one—when we're rushing, the most important thing we can do is slow down.

Let this month's mindfulness practices help you slow down.

March

"He who fears something gives it power over him."

—MOORISH PROVERB

When I was little and would stay at Sissy and Papa's house with my brother, we stayed in my cousin Teny's room. She was older and had already moved away from home.

Every single time, Mickey would tell me there were monsters in the closet. To this day, I can't sleep in a room with a closet door open. Irrational? Yes.

So I know the fears we have feel real, even when we intellectually know they are irrational. And I also know that to fear is to give our power away to something else—whether a closet door or something bigger. What we resist always grows in size.

Morning: What do you fear? Make a list of your fears today.

Evening: Reclaim your power. Focus on one of those fears and make plans to do it anyway—if not today, then soon.

March 1

Catch someone who is falling.

"How it felt to have the world moving beneath me, a hand gripping mine, knowing if I fell, at least I wouldn't do it alone."

—SARAH DESSEN

It is so easy to feel alone. To feel shame when things are falling apart and to keep it all in. To feel like we are falling.

We all need someone to break our fall sometimes. We need someone to pay attention, someone who can tell when we're on the edge of falling, someone who can catch us.

Reach out your hand.

Be that person for someone today.

Morning: Who in your circle could use a hand gripping theirs today?

Evening: How did it feel to break someone's fall? How can you let others in to help you?

March 2

Use your inner compass.

"*Within the mind, there is yet another mind. That mind within the mind: It is an awareness that precedes words.*"

—NEI-YEH, TRANSLATED BY HAROLD D. ROTH

You know.

You *know*.

Now trust that you know.

You know things you cannot explain. Let that intuition be enough. Stop searching for words.

Morning: Pay attention to your gut reactions to people and situations today. Just make a note of your reactions. Practice simply noticing what you notice without judgment.

Evening: What did you discover about your inner compass?

March 3

"You may not remember the time you let me go first. Or the time you dropped back to tell me it wasn't that far to go. Or the time you waited at the crossroads for me to catch up. You may not remember any of those, but I do and this is what I have to say to you: 'Today, no matter what it takes, we ride home together.'"

—BRIAN ANDREAS

It can be so lonely trying to move the rock all by ourselves. There's a time for that, yes. But we can do so, so much more together, knowing that someone is watching out for us, and we them. We can help each other in such small, yet significant ways—the only requirement is to be fully present to another person. There is a beautiful human circle that is created by that kind of attentiveness.

Morning: Whose circle of attentiveness are you in? How are you participating in it?

Evening: Look back at today's quote—who has been there for you, letting you go first or waiting at the crossroads for you? Let them know you remember.

March 4

"To live content with small means; to seek elegance rather than luxury, and refinement rather than fashion; to be worthy, not respectable, and wealthy, not, rich; to listen to stars and birds, babes and sages, with open heart; to study hard; to think quietly, act frankly, talk gently, await occasions, hurry never; in a word, to let the spiritual, unbidden and unconscious, grow up through the common—this is my symphony."

—WILLIAM HENRY CHANNING

Read that quote again, slowly. Aloud.

What is *your* simple symphony?

Morning: Today, let the spiritual grow up through the common in your life. In whatever form that takes for you.

Evening: Are you content with small means? Would you like to be?

March 5

*"Don't judge each day by the harvest you reap
but by the seeds that you plant."*

—ROBERT LOUIS STEVENSON

My friend Lee would go even further. She says gardening is putting a ten-cent plant into a ten-dollar hole. It's the ground we have to focus on and prepare for the best possible harvest, she says. But most of us put all our energy into the plant—the thing we can see—or what we might harvest, the outcome.

Turn your attention to the soil instead. It has to be worked, cultivated, turned, fed. What conditions for success have you provided for the seeds you want to plant?

Morning: Metaphorically, what do you want to plant and harvest in your life?

Evening: What are your "soil" conditions? What needs to change about the ground into which you are going to plant those seeds?

March 6

"The most powerful relationship you will ever have is the relationship with yourself."

—STEVE MARABOLI

Do you love yourself?

Did you know it's not only okay to love yourself, but necessary?

Love is an inside job. Start there.

Morning: Notice the messages you give yourself today—are they loving ones? Do you express compassion toward yourself the way you do toward others? Do you say things to yourself you would never say to a loved one?

Evening: How do you demonstrate your love for yourself? How do you not?

March 7

"Don't follow a trend. Follow your heart."

—KRIST NOVOSELIC

It is so easy to follow others, do what they do, reach for success in a way prescribed by gurus. They are successful! They will tell us what to do! They will save us!

It is so much more meaningful to follow your own heart. Sure, there are dips and valleys in this heart path, but they are *your* dips and valleys and they are there to teach you.

And if you don't know what your heart is telling you, or where it wants to go, that's okay. Take a deep breath. Slow down enough to hear it. This may take years. And that's okay too.

Where is your heart leading you?

Morning: Take a moment this morning before you enter the fray of the day to sit with your hand on your heart and feel it pump. This alone is a miracle! Just sit and feel it for a few minutes.

Evening: How many heartbeats did you have today? A lot. Thank each one, building up your gratitude for the lessons of your heart until you are ready to listen to it.

March 8

"The process of discovering your fearless self is of refinement, not adding."

—STEVE MARABOLI

Leo Tolstoy has said that "truth, like gold, is to be obtained not by its growth, but by washing away from it all that is not gold." A process of refinement.

Our first impulse is to add what we don't have, isn't it? What happens if we stop that process?

What non-gold can you wash away today?

Morning: Pay attention today to what is "essential" and what is not. In what ways can you start shedding those nonessentials?

Evening: What is your gold?

March 9

"Dance, when you're broken open. Dance, if you've torn the bandage off. Dance in the middle of the fighting. Dance in your blood. Dance when you're perfectly free."

—RUMI

Did you know dancing is really good for you? By increasing the number of neural pathways, dancing provides your brain with multiple ways to access information, instead of just one way.

If we put on our boogie shoes while we make breakfast, for example, our brains are going to age better, not to mention how great it feels. Imagine if we dance every day, even for a little bit?

Morning: Put on your favorite music today and dance for five minutes!

Evening: How did your morning dance feel? Can you do it tomorrow too?

March 10

"All that is important is this one moment in movement.
Make the moment important, vital, and worth living.
Do not let it slip away unnoticed and unused."

—MARTHA GRAHAM

A simple message: Move it or lose it. And give up the all-or-nothing thinking. I used to tell my trainer, Michael, that I was going to work out an hour a day while on business travel. He knew—and I knew—that wasn't going to happen. I would be exhausted, getting into hotel rooms at midnight from a long day on planes—and it just wasn't going to happen.

So because I couldn't exercise for an hour, I reasoned that I might as well just eat some chocolate lava cake. He asked me one day: "How about changing your goal?" It was as if he had stabbed me, the thought was so alien. "Change my goal? That's crazy talk. That's giving up."

I changed my goal to walking for ten minutes a day. Achievable in any travel day, a commitment, and a choice toward health that I could celebrate every day.

Morning: How can you incorporate movement into your day today? Not "how can you do a fitness routine for an hour today?"

Evening: How does it feel to consciously move?

March 11

"Think of all the beauty still left around you and be happy."

—ANNE FRANK

Happy is not simple-minded. Happy is not oblivious. Happy is not Pollyanna-ish. Happy is aware, and joyous by choice in the face of tragedy and hardship. And you know what? Happy just feels great. Are there people in your life who drag you down? And are there people who make you feel happy? Spend more time with that second group.

Morning: How can you hang out with happy today?

Evening: Are there unhappy people in your life? How can you reduce your exposure to them or minimize how you let them affect you?

March 12

"Everything has beauty, but not everyone sees it."

—CONFUCIUS

Beauty is simple. It is everywhere. In the curve of that coffee mug's handle. In the sun on trees. In the worn wood on your front porch. In the plant that died because you went away for a long weekend and forgot to water it again. In your own eyes, however tired they might be.

Look for beauty and you will see it.

Look.

See.

Morning: Take photos of the beauty you see today.

Evening: Look at your photos from today. How does revisiting that beauty feel to you? What does it invoke in you?

March 13

"We are what we believe we are!"

—C. S. LEWIS

You are full of magic and sparkle. Yes, you. Is that so hard to see?

Even on days when the sky is gray and people are mean-spirited, you are still amazing. Even when you are cranky and mean-spirited yourself, you are still amazing. Have you ever seen a tiny baby and thought, "What a miracle!" That's what I'm talking about—you are that baby.

Because being amazing is not contingent on other people or conditions. *Can you remember that today, you amazing human?*

Morning: Remind yourself throughout this day that you are amazing, that you are bigger and more amazing than your circumstance.

Evening: Go to bed knowing how amazing you are. Feel it.

"In truth, there is enormous space in which to live our everyday lives."

—PEMA CHÖDRÖN

Our everyday lives are so potent. The soil is so rich in the everyday.

So often we seek more fertile ground—that greener space on the other side of the fence. Where we fail to thrive and where we falter in our appreciation of the everyday is in this urge to be "there" and not "here." What happens if we focus on our everyday lives right where we are instead?

Morning: Take some time to notice your "here" on this day—the shape of the trees, the feeling you have when you see the sky. Notice what you notice.

Evening: Tend your native soil, the ground under your feet. What did you notice today in feeling "here"?

March 15

"If it feels weird, it is weird. Trust your gut."

—JAMIE BELL

In a world hell-bent on measurement and statistics and proof, we often disregard the best barometer we have: our gut. Reconnect to your body; learn from the neck down.

Your body is smarter than you. Listen to it today.

Morning: What is your body trying to tell you? How long has it been trying to tell you that?

Evening: How can you best hear what your body has to say? How can you best honor your body?

March 16

"If we take care of the moments, the years will take care of themselves."

—MARIA EDGEWORTH

Author Annie Dillard has written that how we spend our days is how we spend our lives. It's all incremental. An arc of a life is built day by day until—*poof*—you wake up and you're fifty-four and wonder where all those moments went. Because it's those moments that count. And yet we spend so much time in either the past or the future, don't we?

Morning: Practice being fully in each moment today, not in the past or the future, the now.

Evening: How did that feel? How can being in the "now" help you?

March 17

Lighten the load.

"Besides the noble art of getting things done, there is the noble art of leaving things undone. The wisdom of life consists in the elimination of nonessentials."

—LIN YUTANG

Let something go. Could perfectionism take a hike?
    Look at your "to do" list. Now make a "don't do" list.

Morning: What can remain undone today?

Evening: What can remain undone tomorrow? And the next day? Let something go.

"Thus Gotama [Buddha] walked toward the town to gather alms, and the two samanas recognized him solely by the perfection of his repose, by the calmness of his figure, in which there was no trace of seeking, desiring, imitating, or striving, only light and peace."

—HERMANN HESSE

You are inherently worthy, without seeking, desiring, imitating, or striving.

Today, stop trying so hard. Live with ease; extend loving grace to yourself.

Morning: Let your figure be calm today, without seeking.

Evening: If you focus on being only light and peace without striving or desiring, how does that feel?

March 19

*"In the beginner's mind there are many possibilities;
in the expert's mind, there are few."*

—SHUNRYU SUZUKI

I'm taking old-time fiddle lessons. It is an instrument about which I know nothing. I feel like a child with it, exploring and not knowing, and yet battling my desire to know, to get better. What deflects me from a posture of not knowing? The desire to know in order to feel in control, smart, sophisticated, well rehearsed. By doing that, I am shutting down possibilities. Is there a balance between the two? Can we "not know" in order to get to the deeper layer of what insecurities lie within that?

Morning: Try not knowing today. Step back from your expert's mind. Ask more questions. Listen to the answers.

Evening: How does it feel to "not know"?

March 20

"Even in the familiar there can be surprise and wonder."

—TIERNEY GEARON

We separate the ordinary from the extraordinary in so many ways, discounting the one and wishing for the other. They are the same.

Find surprise and wonder in the most familiar things around you today. It is there. Share that surprise with others—is a plant blooming? Share it! Take photos of it, explore it. Allow yourself to be surprised by it.

Morning: Create surprise for someone today by showing up for them. And allow yourself to be surprised by your ordinary life.

Evening: What does surprise and wonder feel like in your body?

March 21

> *"To be fully alive, fully human, and completely awake is to be continually thrown out of the nest. To live fully is to be always in no-man's-land, to experience each moment as completely new and fresh. To live is to be willing to die over and over again."*
>
> —PEMA CHÖDRÖN

What does it mean to be fully alive? I think it means to feel everything you feel, without asking "why" too much. We live so much in our heads—let's let ourselves be fully embodied instead.

Focus on feeling today.

Fly from the nest.

Morning: Focus on how the air feels on your skin today. Stand in a breeze and feel it fully. Don't worry about the direction of the wind or whether you need a jacket. Just feel it.

Evening: How can you continue to allow yourself to be fully embodied and in the world?

March 22

"*This is what I believe: That I am I. That my soul is a dark forest. That my known self will never be more than a little clearing in the forest. That gods, strange gods, come forth from the forest into the clearing of my known self, and then go back. That I must have the courage to let them come and go. That I will never let mankind put anything over me, but that I will try always to recognize and submit to the gods in me and the gods in other men and women. There is my creed.*"

—D. H. LAWRENCE

We need a spaciousness in us. We need to honor that little clearing in the forest, sweep it free of pine needles, let the light in. Clear the ground, clear ground.

Morning: How are you creating spaciousness in your little clearing in the forest?

Evening: Sometimes clearing ground requires divestiture. What can you let go of? A thing, or a story about yourself, or something else?

March 23

"Tell me, what is it you plan to do / with your one wild and precious life?"

—MARY OLIVER

I love the idea that I have a wild and precious life. Even just reframing it in that way imbues it with a glory well beyond dirty laundry and trying to decide on what to cook for dinner.

Well, depending on the nature of your spirituality and religious beliefs, there may be more lives for you, but this is the only one you have in this moment. Cherish it. Treat it as if it is wild and precious. Because it is. It truly is.

Morning: Let this be your mantra today: "I love my one wild and precious life. Let everything I do today reflect that love."

Evening: How did that mantra change your experience of your life today?

"I have to figure out why I worked at a job I hated for years. I have to find out why I can't see what everyone else sees in me. I don't feel beautiful. When I look in the mirror, I never saw beautiful. I can't see me and I need to be able to do that. I need to find out what I'm like and what I want. I have to be comfortable in my own skin before I can be in a relationship the way you want."

—CHRISTINE FEEHAN

When you hear the words "love more," do you think "love others more"? Or do you think "love myself more"? Start with that second one. Without it, you can't get to the first one.

Morning: Today, wear a rubber band on one wrist. Every time you see it, think to yourself, "I love myself." Get over the self-consciousness of thinking that. Just allow yourself to do it.

Evening: What did you discover? Wear that rubber band as long as necessary.

March 25

"This life is yours. Take the power to choose what you want to do and do it well. Take the power to love what you want in life and love it honestly. Take the power to walk in the forest and be a part of nature. Take the power to control your own life. No one else can do it for you. Take the power to make your life happy."

—SUSAN POLIS SCHUTZ

We live out loud on the Interwebs, don't we? But sometimes rocking on with our bad selves is private, quiet, and beautifully unspoken. It doesn't always need to be showy and loud. Happy is often a whisper, a gorgeous whisper.

Rock on, quiet pilgrim.

Morning: What power do you want to reclaim? As you go through your day, own that power.

Evening: Revolutions can be quiet. What quiet revolution do you want to start in your own life?

March 26

"All you have to do is to pay attention; lessons always arrive when you are ready, and if you can read the signs, you will learn everything you need to know in order to take the next step."

—PAULO COELHO

You know how sometimes when you're speeding along the interstate and there's a sign up ahead, the lettering can be pretty tiny and maybe in an ugly typeface? You know what you have to do to read the sign?

That's right.

Slow down.

Morning: What signs are you seeing, but ignoring?

Evening: What signs are you missing because you are moving too fast?

March 27

"We need 4 hugs a day for survival. We need 8 hugs a day for maintenance. We need 12 hugs a day for growth. . . ."

—VIRGINIA SATIR

One of the most remarkable moments in my life was centered around free hugs. I can still remember the moment when my daughter Emma walked into the center of Main Street with her "Free Hugs" sign. And she stood there, shy Emma, quiet and with her feet together. People passed her by. My heart jumped for her, wanting someone to take her up on her offer of a free hug, wanting someone to know how hard it was for her to do that.

And then a swirl of purple ran from the left and hugged Emma, picking her up and swirling her. A beautiful woman with gray dreadlocks was the first. And there were many more after that.

It takes one to start. Be that one.

Morning: Try to give at least four hugs today. Aim for twelve. If you are alone, hug yourself. Really.

Evening: What does it mean to hug others? If you aren't a hugger, how can you translate that connection into another form?

March 28

"You are an explorer, and you represent our species, and the greatest good you can do is to bring back a new idea, because our world is endangered by the absence of good ideas. Our world is in crisis because of the absence of consciousness."

—TERENCE MCKENNA

Be conscious. Explore. Please bring back a new idea today.

Morning: As you go through your day today, notice when you are merely passing along the ideas of others—like those automatic "shares" on Facebook. Instead, put one of your own ideas into the mix today.

Evening: Don't stop exploring. Ever.

"When people hurt you over and over, think of them like sandpaper. They may scratch and hurt you a bit, but in the end, you end up polished and they end up useless."

—ANONYMOUS

When we get hurt by others, we have a choice: We can welcome them into our lives and hearts where they can continue to poison us, or we can be thankful we are not them and that we don't see the world the way they do, we can say a silent "wow," and then we can let them go.

Morning: Shake them off. The weight to carry them along with us is too great.

Evening: Let yourself be polished by the ways in which others hurt you. Remember them as sandpaper.

"About all you can do in life is be who you are. Some people will love you for you. Most will love you for what you can do for them, and some won't like you at all."

—RITA MAE BROWN

In the past year, I learned that transparency and honesty are not the same thing. That I like things on a very human scale. That I love to hug people and be hugged. That fat is a protective device. That I am invested in stories that no longer serve me. That I want to write more, again. That I need help. That we are all actively dying. That people are human and humans are animals and we are all only one step away from making animal decisions. That judging people by their actions is not all we can do. That I am always in choice. That kindness is always the best option. That saying yes means saying yes to myself, which often looks and sounds like "no" to others. That I miss making art. That I miss my freckles. That I miss people. That death can be a relief. That illness is for stepping into. That Tess is doing the best she can. That I could do better. That I need to simply come as I am.

Morning: How can you simply come as you are, laying down all the protective devices and deflections?

Evening: How does it feel to put down your clever and pick up your ordinary? What keeps you from doing it?

March 31

This feels like a month of growth to me, a time to reinvest in ourselves. In the hemisphere in which I live, it is a moment of blooming forth from the earth—the air feels kinder to us in these days.

What newness can you invest in this month? Do you need a do-over? This is the month for that.

Start anew.

April

"When I loved myself enough, I began leaving whatever wasn't healthy. This meant people, jobs, my own beliefs and habits—anything that kept me small. My judgment called it disloyal. Now I see it as self-loving."

—KIM MCMILLEN

What is keeping you small?

    What people?

    What jobs?

    What beliefs of yours?

    What habits of yours?

    Today, show love to yourself by beginning to leave whatever isn't healthy. Even small steps in the other direction will empower you.

Morning: As you go through your day today, acknowledge and simply notice what you feel is keeping you small. Notice it without judgment—just notice.

Evening: Did you discover anything today? What would you like to leave behind from what you noticed?

April 1

"Life is a process of becoming, a combination of states we have to go through. Where people fail is that they wish to elect a state and remain in it. This is a kind of death."

—ANAÏS NIN

It is so easy to love *being,* and so hard to love *becoming*—that messy place we have to journey through. And yet, life flows and in flowing, changes.

We can fight it, resist it, or allow ourselves to flow with it. Fighting change takes energy we could spend on living instead. Resisting change makes its impact all the larger—it grows in proportion to our resistance. Flowing with change acknowledges our agility, our ability to have waves crash over us and still survive.

Morning: What change can you let go of your need to resist today?

Evening: What does it feel in your body to let go of fighting and resistance?

"The really important kind of freedom involves attention, and awareness, and discipline, and effort, and being able truly to care about other people and to sacrifice for them, over and over, in myriad petty little unsexy ways, every day."

—DAVID FOSTER WALLACE

What does it really mean to show up for someone else? Not the big moments, but those small, unglamorous ones. Find out today.

Morning: In what petty little unsexy ways can you show up for other people today?

Evening: How does it feel to show up for someone else? Can you let others show up for you in the same way?

April 3

"There's never enough of the stuff you can't get enough of."

—PATRICK H. T. DOYLE

Maybe what you need is less.

Morning: What can you give away?

Evening: How does it feel to need less?

April 4

"Clouds come floating into my life, no longer to carry rain or usher storm, but to add color to my sunset sky."

—RABINDRANATH TAGORE

This day is ending tonight at midnight, as do all days.

To honor what this day was and to open space for what will be tomorrow, sit quietly today for ten minutes (or longer).

Quiet your mind. Rest those skittering thoughts and worries. Let them float across your field of vision and disappear like puffy clouds.

They'll likely come back into your field of vision again, and that's okay. Clouds are beautiful.

Morning: Find time in your day to watch the sky today.

Evening: Were you able to find time to quiet your mind today? If not, can you tomorrow?

April 5

"Any intelligent fool can make things bigger, more complex, and more violent. It takes a touch of genius—and a lot of courage—to move in the opposite direction."

—E. F. SCHUMACHER

Occam's razor is a tenet I come back to over and over again: a principle that entities should not be multiplied needlessly; the simplest of two competing theories is to be preferred. For example, when I have a bad headache, I go straight for brain tumor as explanation; my husband, John, suggests dehydration as the cause—simple, clear.

I wonder what I can pare down, get my thinking clean about, simplify.

Morning: What thoughts can you simplify today? See if this question helps: What else might be true?

Evening: What thoughts did you let go of today? And which ones will you let go of tomorrow?

April 6

"I have come to accept the feeling of not knowing where I am going. And I have trained myself to love it. Because it is only when we are suspended in mid-air with no landing in sight, that we force our wings to unravel and alas begin our flight. And as we fly, we still may not know where we are going to. But the miracle is in the unfolding of the wings. You may not know where you're going, but you know that so long as you spread your wings, the winds will carry you."

—C. JOYBELL C.

Learning only happens when we don't know. Let's not know more often. *Unfold.*

Morning: Imagine you have wings. Feel them on your back. Unfold them several times today, then fold them back up. (This will do wonders for your posture too!)

Evening: How does it feel to walk around with wings?

April 7

"So at the end of this day, we give thanks / For being betrothed to the unknown."

—JOHN O'DONOHUE

I love the whole idea of desire lines from landscape architecture, those bare paths we wear across the grass even though an "official" concrete path lies nearby. These dirt paths we wear in the ground over time show us where we really want to go. And I know that a new path is made up of many steps over time. Into the unknown. Take one.

Morning: What new path can you take today? Even something as literal as taking a different route to school or work or play today.

Evening: How does it feel to be betrothed to the unknown?

April 8

"All I have is a voice."

—W. H. AUDEN

So many people say, "I need to find my voice."

You know what? You have a voice. You don't need to find it. You just need to use it. *What do you long to say?*

Morning: Say what you long to say today, whether in writing, music, art, or words aloud. Say it.

Evening: What keeps you from speaking in your one true voice?

April 9

"Some of these kids just don't plain know how good they are: how smart and how much they have to say. You can tell them. You can shine that light on them, one human interaction at a time."

—DAVE EGGERS

Sometimes when we hear the word "shine," we think of shining our own light. And that's cool. But I really like Dave Eggers's take on it: Let's shine light on others so they will know they, too, can shine.

Morning: Who can you shine a light on today, one human interaction at a time?

Evening: "Shining a light" can take many forms, such as a personal note, a phone call, an invitation to participate. What are some ways you feel comfortable shining a light on others?

April 10

"To say you have no choice is to relieve yourself of responsibility."

—PATRICK NESS

We are so used to saying "I can't" that it never occurs to us that what is more truthful is "I choose not to." Saying "I can't" takes the burden off of us, but it isn't truthful most of the time. We are choosing not to, instead.

What happens if we stop abdicating our personal responsibilities to circumstance?

It's true—you can't always choose your circumstances. But you are always in choice about how you *are* in those circumstances. Choose well. Because that choice is entirely up to you. And, over time, those choices become the story of your life.

Morning: Today, replace "I can't" with "I choose not to" and see what happens.

Evening: Tomorrow, try this out: Replace "I have to" with "I choose to."

April 11

"Always say 'yes' to the present moment. What could be more futile, more insane, than to create inner resistance to what already is? What could be more insane than to oppose life itself, which is now and always now? Surrender to what is. Say 'yes' to life—and see how life suddenly starts working for you rather than against you."

—ECKHART TOLLE

This is a great question: "What could be more futile, more insane, than to create inner resistance to what already is?" And yet we do, we do.

Morning: Today, pay attention to moments of inner resistance, and surrender to what is.

Evening: What is your biggest obstacle to embracing what already is?

April 12

"Time to live, time to lie, time to laugh, and time to die. Take it easy, baby. Take it as it comes."

—JIM MORRISON

Inhale deeply while you think to yourself (or say aloud): "Hello, moment." Exhale deeply while thinking or saying: "I am here."

Hello, moment. I am here.

Easy now, baby. Take it as it comes today. Keep breathing yourself into the moment today.

Morning: Start your day with three repetitions of "Hello, moment / I am here," breathing in the moment and out with "I am here." Repeat silently to yourself as needed throughout the day.

Evening: As you end this day, reflect on how this grounding helped you—what did you discover in breathing in the moments today?

April 13

We sit on the sidelines far too often, cheering others on or complaining about the referees or chiding someone for missing the shot. We scream and shout and sit in anticipation of the next move of those on the field.

Step into the game today.

Morning: How can you participate instead of watching today?

Evening: What kind of player do you want to be?

April 14

*"But Piglet is so small that he slips into a pocket, where
it is very comfortable to feel him when you are not quite
sure whether twice seven is twelve or twenty-two."*

—A. A. MILNE

I hope you can find a way to be a little Piglet for someone today.
Tuck yourself into their pocket to comfort them. Just be there.

Morning: Choose someone to show up for today. Be there for
them in an inconspicuous way, like Piglet.

Evening: How did it feel to give comfort in that way?

April 15

"It's the action, not the fruit of the action, that's important. You have to do the right thing. It may not be in your power, may not be in your time, that there'll be any fruit. But that doesn't mean you stop doing the right thing. You may never know what results come from your action. But if you do nothing, there will be no result."

—MAHATMA GANDHI

Here's the deal.

You make a difference in ways you can never know.

For all the people who might tell you what a difference you make, there are so very many more who don't say it, but feel it.

It might not seem that way. But it is.

Trust this truth. Live your life as if you fully believe it, even on those days when you do not.

Morning: Find someone who needs love and support and offer that in a way they can hear it, feel it, know it. It is the best gift we can give, now and forever. You make a difference.

Evening: Make a difference every day by acting on things that matter.

April 16

You know the answer.

Some days it really doesn't feel that way. It seems like everyone else knows, but you don't.

Some days it's really easy to doubt yourself, to wonder where to look for answers.

Some days it's too easy to ask "why" you feel a certain way—asking "why" can invalidate the fact that you *do* feel that way.

Some days it feels like you need to travel to Oz to find what you're looking for.

But you don't.

All right there, inside you. Be still long enough to hear what your heart has to say.

Morning: What is the question?

Evening: What do you know that you don't allow yourself to fully know?

April 17

"Don't postpone joy."

—LAUREY MASTERTON

Don't postpone happy.

Don't postpone joy.

Don't postpone eating well.

Don't postpone moving your body.

It is no badge of honor to put yourself last, work too hard, eat on the run, sit too long, be too important to play.

Don't postpone feeling good right now.

Morning: Today, simply notice all the ways in which you postpone joy. Don't judge yourself for it—just notice it.

Evening: Tomorrow, notice those same ways in which you postpone joy, and surprise yourself by breaking the pattern.

April 18

"The wound is the place where the Light enters you."

—RUMI

It is easy to feel like we're broken. So many people are willing to tell us we are. We have pathologized being human. Being human *means* imperfection. It means discomfort as well as joy. It means we screw up and make messes sometimes. It means we hurt as well as laugh. Does that mean we're broken? No, that means we're human.

Beautifully, messily, chaotically, fantastically, fully human. Those cracks? As Leonard Cohen tells us, "There is a crack in everything. That's how the light gets in."

You're not broken, and you don't need to be fixed.

Morning: Today, imagine light pouring in through all the places life has cracked you open. Imagine light pouring out into the world from those cracks as well.

Evening: How did it feel to be a vessel of light today?

April 19

"You're alive. Do something. The directive in life, the moral imperative was so uncomplicated. It could be expressed in single words, not complete sentences. It sounded like this: Look. Listen. Choose. Act."

—BARBARA HALL

We've all heard this before: *Be part of the solution*. And yet many of us don't step up. Sure, we pass along petitions and posters and shocking news stories on Facebook and Twitter, but often that's the extent of it. Perhaps it's because there is so, so much that needs doing. Perhaps it's because we believe that surely someone else is doing something about it. Perhaps it's because we believe that someone more qualified will step in. All of those things might be true. But they also may not be true.

Morning: Today, look and listen.

Evening: Tomorrow, choose and act.

April 20

"How we spend our days is, of course, how we spend our lives."

—ANNIE DILLARD

This is the time of your life. Some of you are saying, "YES! IT IS!" And others of you are saying, "God, I hope not." Regardless of your first reaction to this daily rock, this very moment is the *only* time of your life. It's the only one you have. The next one? Not guaranteed. What happens if we opt for the first reaction, "YES! IT IS!" every single day, even the hard days, the despairing ones, the panicky and hopeless ones? Especially those. Have the time of your life today.

Morning: Pay attention to how you spend your day today.

Evening: Was this day the time of your life? If it wasn't, how could tomorrow be more closely aligned with how you want to spend your life?

April 21

"I am learning all the time. The tombstone will be my diploma."

—EARTHA KITT

I'm on a quest to learn something new every day. Not big things, necessarily. Not exhausting things that take a lot of time and practice to master. Just little things. Like how to pronounce "err" correctly. Or how much ⁵/₈ of a cup is when you're baking. Or how to translate what you value into the actions you take. Or how important it is to drop everything when someone you love wants to talk to you. Or how to say a simple hello in three languages. An agile mind that stays agile—that's at the top of my bucket list.

Morning: What will you learn today?

Evening: What will your life look like if learning is near the top of your priorities?

April 22

"He who would travel happily must travel light."

—ANTOINE DE SAINT-EXUPÉRY

My daughter Emma is getting ready for a six-week study trip this summer, so traveling light is front of mind for us right now—along with memories of my own college travels with a backpack. (And living light is a big part of my internal conversation these days too.) I've written tips for travel before. I'm rethinking them to be even simpler. Certainly lighter. Both in terms of what you carry with you physically and also what you carry emotionally. Shed. Travel light. Pack only what you can easily carry. You won't need the rest.

Morning: What's in all those bags you're carrying around? Unpack them.

Evening: How can you travel lighter in your life?

April 23

"Every time you smile at someone, it is an action of love, a gift to that person, a beautiful thing."

—MOTHER TERESA

When I travel, I play a game in airports where everyone looks serious and stressed and late or disconnected. It's a really simple game. And it takes my mind off my own delayed flights. I just count the number of people I can make smile or laugh. It becomes a great adventure, a direction of intention. I love the victories! Even just the small, tentative grins, and especially the big belly laughs. Some people resist smiling, and that's okay. Others? A connection through that beautiful uplift of a mouth, a crinkle of the eyes, and sometimes even the noise of laughter in the din of the terminal.

Morning: How many people can you make smile today?

Evening: How did that feel?

April 24

*"It is always important to know when something has reached
its end. Closing circles, shutting doors, finishing chapters,
it doesn't matter what we call it; what matters is to leave
in the past those moments in life that are over."*

—PAULO COELHO

You are here now.
> There is only one way to go from here.
> Take a step.
> Go forward.

Morning: What moments do you need to leave in the past?

Evening: What step forward did you take today?

April 25

"Detachment means letting go and nonattachment means simply letting be."

—STEPHEN LEVINE

When I travel, I carry daily rocks with me and leave them in airports and hotels for others to find.

At first, I have to admit I wanted to see someone find the little rock message, just to experience the joy of that moment of wonder. And then I realized that by leaving the rock to be found like a sweet serendipity, I had made my strong offer. I didn't need to know the outcome.

The more I've been able to detach from outcome, the freer I have become. When I write a book, by the time it is published, my work is long since done and my job is to keep writing, not look at Amazon.com rankings or reviews. When I parent, my job is to open space for my kids to walk into and through, and I have to let go of the outcome, knowing I have done my part.

If we can detach from outcome, we can make truer, more honest, stronger offers.

Morning: What outcome do you want or need to detach from?

Evening: How does it feel to give up attachment to outcome? Does it open space for you to make your strongest offer?

April 26

"If someone comes along and shoots an arrow into your heart, it's fruitless to stand there and yell at the person. It would be much better to turn your attention to the fact that there's an arrow in your heart. . . ."

—PEMA CHÖDRÖN

I've been thinking a lot about forgiveness. And about letting go deeply. Why is it so hard to forgive and let go? Is it because we are right and they are wrong? Do we hold so tight to our "rightness" and our need to have that "rightness" validated that we stop ourselves from moving forward? Do we carry a heavy burden around with us when forgiveness would lighten our load? This is important: Ultimately, we don't forgive others because *they* deserve it or need it. We forgive because *we* deserve it and need it.

Morning: How can you turn your attention to your own heart today?

Evening: Whom do you need or want to forgive and let go?

April 27

"Sometimes you just have to jump in a mud puddle because it's there. Never get so old that you forget about having fun."

—TOM GIAQUINTO

You will never have all the information you need to make a well-informed decision.

You will never make the perfect decision with all the information in the world.

You will always have the option to mitigate the disadvantages of a decision that no longer serves you (i.e., change your mind).

Chances are, the decision you are facing is not the last decision you'll ever make.

The mud will dry.

Fling yourself in!

Morning: Notice the impulses you feel today that you squash and don't act on. Consider why (and how) you stop yourself.

Evening: Tomorrow, find one "mud puddle" to fling yourself into.

April 28

"We're all just walking each other home."

—RAM DASS

Sometimes the you-know-what hits the fan. Like the week of the bombing at the Boston Marathon in 2013, locking down the whole city. That same week there was an earthquake in China, deadly explosions in Texas, floods in the Midwest, tornado warnings, and more.

May we all remember that we're just walking each other home. And may we make that walk hand in hand. May we remember the ways in which we pull together in times of crisis and never let that go. May we also remember our fellow human beings in places of conflict where bombings are an everyday occurrence, every day, each day. May we walk with them in their terror as well.

Morning: Who can you "walk home" today, hand in hand?

Evening: What does walking hand in hand with the world look like for you?

April 29

"There is a primal reassurance in being touched, in knowing that someone else, someone close to you, wants to be touching you. There is a bone-deep security that goes with the brush of a human hand, a silent, reflex-level affirmation that someone is near, that someone cares."

—JIM BUTCHER

People near you are hurting.
    Stay available.
    Stay close.

Morning: What does "stay available" look like to you? How agile is your life?

Evening: Who is available for you?

April 30

What will this new month bring?

What will you bring to this new month? That's the better question.

Life doesn't happen to us—we participate in it, sometimes by playing a passive role and wondering what will happen: "What will happen to me this month?" And sometimes by acknowledging that we are in charge and that our interaction in our life is what makes things happen: "What am I bringing to this life?"

Bring something to life this month.

May

"The mistake is thinking that there can be an antidote to the uncertainty."

—DAVID LEVITHAN

Knowing keeps us from learning.

Knowing keeps us from true dialogue.

Knowing keeps us clever and separated from experience.

Being unsure opens us up to discovery.

Being unsure allows us to listen to understand, not listen just to reply.

Being unsure plops us right in the middle of what is and what we are experiencing.

Be unsure.

Morning: How does it feel in your body if you are unsure? How could you come to appreciate and love that feeling—and seek it out rather than endure it?

Evening: What kind of a listener are you? One who listens to reply or to understand?

May I

"Letting go doesn't mean that you don't care about someone anymore. It's just realizing that the only person you really have control over is yourself."

—DEBORAH REBER

Sometimes life provides us with circumstances we don't like and don't want.

This provides us with a decision point: Either we can invest in our yearning (what we long for) or we can invest in the obstacles that keep us from that yearning (what we think is stopping us).

We can either accept what is, or we can change our response to it, even if we can't change the circumstances themselves.

The only person we can change is ourself.

Morning: Being in "drama" is a place of exhaustion, of bemoaning what *is* by blaming. What happens if you approach *what is* from a place of choice?

Evening: Which will you choose tomorrow? Investing in your yearning or in the obstacles?

May 2

"Smiling is the way the soul says hello. Obviously a frown means goodbye. Is there a word halfway between hello and goodbye? Because that's what my soul is saying right now."

—JAROD KINTZ

It doesn't cost anything.

It isn't as awkward as it might seem.

It can bring a smile to your face, and to theirs.

Today, say hello to people you see in the grocery store, at the library, on Main Street. Say hello to people you know and don't know. Say hello to connection, so often lost in the hurry, the fear, the hiding.

Say hello.

Morning: Say hello to everyone you meet today.

Evening: How did that feel? What did you discover?

May 3

"If I were not a physicist, I would probably be a musician. I often think in music. I live my daydreams in music. I see my life in terms of music."

—ALBERT EINSTEIN

There is a deep, resonant music in your bones, your blood-stream, every beat of your heart.

There is a rhythm to your life, a calling, a coursing, a fortissimo song some days, a dolce melody others, a discordant harmony the next.

Can you feel it?

Can you hear it?

Are you allowing enough silence into your life to be able to hear what your life is saying?

Today, incorporate quiet into your life. Listen, hear.

Morning: Listen for rhythms today. The water sprinkler, the beating of your heart, the song of the birds, the wind in the trees. What rhythms do you hear when you listen?

Evening: Imagine your life as a piece of music each day. Play it with all your heart.

May 4

Admit
mistakes
with grace

"We are all mistaken sometimes; sometimes we do wrong things, things that have bad consequences. But it does not mean we are evil, or that we cannot be trusted ever afterward."

—ALISON CROGGON

When I was in the third grade, someone noticed a puddle of pee around my desk. Even though my dress was wet and I was sitting in urine, I swore it wasn't me; the shame was too great. We all have our own unique responses to making mistakes, many of which are patterns that started very young. And each of us, still, can learn to admit mistakes with grace and break those unhealthy patterns.

I learned that from Tami Taylor, the coach's wife on *Friday Night Lights*. When a mistake was made on the show, she voiced it and talked to the people involved. Lessons were learned, and they moved on.

Morning: What is your pattern about admitting you were wrong?

Evening: What healthier pattern would you like to practice?

May 5

*"We all dream of being exactly what we are—
powerful, beautiful, and worthy."*

—VIRONIKA TUGALEVA

I was recently asked to be a distinguished lecturer at a university—
and it nearly did me in. Why? Because I had created a story of
who I needed to be in that setting—more serious, more aca-
demic, more . . . something I was not. The imposition of this
story-of-my-own-making kept me paralyzed for a very long
time as I prepared for the speech, and had an impact on the
speech itself, I'm afraid. Why is it so hard to see ourselves as
powerful, beautiful, and worthy just as we are? Why do we leave
it to others to define us?

Morning: Make this your mantra today: "I am powerful, beautiful, and worthy just as I am." Say this to yourself on the hour
every hour today. Set an alarm if you need to.

Evening: How did that mantra feel today? How can you remind
yourself of this tomorrow and beyond?

May 6

"One hand I extend into myself, the other toward others."

—DEJAN STOJANOVIĆ

By extending an open hand, we not only can give, but also receive. But when our hands are closed, grasping onto something—an object, a belief, a relationship—we cannot give or receive. Life is about flow, not stopping the flow. What I love about this quote is that we often forget to extend one hand to ourselves—this is a reminder to do that first.

Morning: How can you open up your hand and extend it to yourself today?

Evening: What did you discover about loosening your grip? How did it feel to extend an open hand to yourself?

May 7

*"You should never be surprised by or feel the need to explain
why any physical system is in a high entropy state."*

—BRIAN GREENE

When socks are missing from my dryer, I blame it on plate tec-
tonics or entropy. There is a constant in our lives, and that is
the move toward chaos. That dining room table you cleared this
morning? It's covered with school folders now, and forks from
breakfast. All those beautiful, spotless rooms on Pinterest?
Nobody lives in them.

I used to avoid answering the door when people stopped
by—the house needed picking up or vacuuming. Not so anymore. Love me, love my dust. The same is true of our lives, not
just our homes. We can't wait for everything to be perfect—it is
always headed for chaos. Jump.

Morning: What entropy can you live with? What entropy can't
you live with?

Evening: How would it feel not to apologize for or explain the
chaos in your life?

May 8

"*How many slams in an old screen door? Depends how loud you shut it. How many slices in a bread? Depends how thin you cut it. How much good inside a day? Depends how good you live 'em. How much love inside a friend? Depends how much you give 'em.*"

—SHEL SILVERSTEIN

It is easy to rely solely on Facebook messages or e-mail to communicate with friends. What's missing are the bits in between the words—the easy laughter, the silence in which you both ponder something, the nuance of voices so familiar to us. Give some love to a friend today, voices mingling and not just on a page.

Morning: Call a friend today. Voice to voice.

Evening: Can you commit to calling a friend once a week? Consistency over times builds relationships. And builds your voice muscle.

May 9

"We have all a better guide in ourselves, if we would attend to it, than any other person can be."

—JANE AUSTEN

You know.

Why don't you trust that you know?

What messages have you received that tell you, "You don't know. Someone else must know better"?

I feel those messages, and fight my way back to my own heart. It is easy to feel you can't trust your own judgment. So many people outside ourselves have "answers" for us. But honey, you've got you. And nobody cares for you like you do. Trust yourself.

Morning: Try to identify the ways in which you have abdicated your own judgment to others. And try to identify the ways in which you have grown to believe you aren't trustworthy.

Evening: What patterns are you noticing? How are those patterns serving you? Do they take you "off the hook," for example? How can you change those patterns?

May 10

"The nitrogen in our DNA, the calcium in our teeth, the iron in our blood, the carbon in our apple pies were made in the interiors of collapsing stars. We are made of starstuff."

—CARL SAGAN

Oh, we look so long for a North Star to steer by.
    When all along, we are our own North Star, starstuff.

Morning: You know how much reverence we give the North Star? Today, give that much reverence to your own wisdom, your own North Star.

Evening: How does it feel to remember you are starstuff, and that you have what you need to steer by?

May 11

"Do stuff. Be clenched, curious. Not waiting for inspiration's shove or society's kiss on your forehead. Pay attention. It's all about paying attention. Attention is vitality. It connects you with others. It makes you eager. Stay eager."

—SUSAN SONTAG

Every moment is a call for attention.

"Mom! Look at this!"

A rainbow watercoloring the sky.

The cardinal at the back feeder, showing red, red.

The hard rains and their impact on the waterfall.

A meeting that has no point.

Protests in the streets.

"Pay attention," the world is saying to you! Whether you answer that call and embrace paying attention and the vitality that comes with it—that's completely up to you.

Morning: How can you remind yourself to pay attention today? For me, it is making notes on index cards that keeps me in a space of mindfulness and attention. It may be different for you.

Evening: Tomorrow—and every day—this same vitality is available to you. Will you embrace it by paying attention to your life in a deeper, richer way?

May 12

"Very little is needed to make a happy life; it is all within yourself in your way of thinking."

—MARCUS AURELIUS

I talked to my mom recently on the phone. In a lull in the conversation, she said, "Life is hard, honey."

I sat, and I listened. And I thought afterward how true that is for her, and many others, because that is the lens through which they have chosen to see the world.

We get to choose, every day, whether to see life as hard or richly faceted. Whether to see difficulties or possibilities. Whether to see boundaries or horizons. We get to choose whether to say, "Life is hard," or "Life is amazing." Even in the worst of circumstances, this is true. We choose.

Morning: Notice your life-speak today—are you choosing "hard" or "enriching," "devastating" or "illuminating"?

Evening: What did you notice about your choices? What will you choose tomorrow?

May 13

"What makes us normal is knowing that we're not normal."

—HARUKI MURAKAMI

My older daughter, Emma, once asked me, "Who gets to say what 'normal' is?"

Who, indeed?

Most of us go through our lives wearing little, invisible umbrella hats. Umbrellas protect us from outside forces, and in this case, on the underneath of my invisible umbrella hat, it says, "Normal." And whatever happens that isn't inside that definition of "normal," is, by definition, "not normal."

We need bigger umbrella hats. Or no hats at all, just humans bumping up against one another realizing there is no "normal."

Morning: Notice your invisible umbrella hat today—what falls outside the realm of "normal" that you have either consciously or unconsciously created in your life? Imagine a person wearing their own invisible umbrella hat looking at you and defining you as "abnormal." How does that feel?

Evening: How can you expand your definition of "normal"?

May 14

> "*When we fully understand the brevity of life, its fleeting joys and unavoidable pains; when we accept the facts that all men and women are approaching an inevitable doom: the consciousness of it should make us more kindly and considerate of each other. This feeling should make men and women use their best efforts to help their fellow travelers on the road, to make the path brighter and easier as we journey on. It should bring a closer kinship, a better understanding, and a deeper sympathy for the wayfarers who must live a common life and die a common death.*"

—CLARENCE DARROW

Consider this day precious.

Consider that you are dying, and that this is one of your last days.

How does that change things?

Because you are dying. And this is one of your last days, no matter how long your life lasts. Just consider this in the way you greet this day, in the way you hold it, in the way you share it with others.

Just consider this.

Morning: Notice how this consideration changes your day today.

Evening: Embrace what you can of this consideration as a daily practice.

May 15

"Modern culture's worship of 'how-to' pragmatism has turned us into instruments of efficiency and commerce—but we're doing more and more about things that mean less and less. We constantly ask how? but rarely why? We use how as a defense—instead of acting on what we know to be of importance, we wait until we've attended one more workshop, read one more book, gotten one more degree. Asking how keeps us safe—instead of being led by our hearts into uncharted territory, we keep our heads down and stick to the map. But we are gaining the world and losing our souls."

—PETER BLOCK

"How" is our modern anthem.

"How can I do that too?" we ask as we pore over Pinterest.

"How did you do that?" we ask on Facebook.

"How" keeps us safe. What happens when we focus on "why," instead, is that we dive into meaningfulness, not busyness.

Morning: Make note of the number of times you say (or start to say) "how" today. Substitute "why" and see what happens. In what ways does that change the conversation (and the focus)?

Evening: Into what kind of uncharted territory would "why" allow your heart to roam?

May 16

Write a
poem with
your life.

*"'You mean you're comparing our lives to a sonnet? A strict
form, but freedom within it?' 'Yes.' Mrs. Whatsit said.
'You're given the form, but you have to write the sonnet
yourself. What you say is completely up to you.'"*

—MADELEINE L'ENGLE

We separate art from life in so many ways. So you don't call
yourself a poet? It doesn't matter—your life is still a poem. What
happens when you see it as one?

First, what do we know about poetry? There are images that
stand in for other things in poems. A window that is dirty might
mean something different from a shiny, clean window. A black
crow appearing on a branch might signify something different from a hummingbird. In such a way, language and image
become a metaphorical architecture—just like in our dreams.

Morning: Pay attention to the images in your life today. Gather
snippets of what you see and experience today.

Evening: Put those snippets together into a "poem." If the
word "poem" seems overwhelming to you, just put those snippets together in an image made from words. In such a way, we
pay more attention to our days, and find threads we might not
otherwise see.

May 17

"To be yourself in a world that is constantly trying to make you something else is the greatest accomplishment."

—RALPH WALDO EMERSON

We listen to so many messages about what we need to do or own or accomplish in order to be successful.

Tess's list for Santa used to be seventy items long. "I need this! I want this!" she would say as she added to the list of complicated, expensive items.

The year we cut the plug on TV, her list went from seventy items to one item: "A red ball."

What if we cut the plug on those messages and focused on what we really want? And on our own definition of success?

Morning: Pay attention to the messages you get today about what you need (or need more of) to be successful, hot, attractive, _____ (fill in the blank with an aspiration).

Evening: From where did these messages come? Which of those pipelines can you close? How reliant are you on those pipelines to tell you what you want or need?

May 18

"Stories are the creative conversion of life itself into a more powerful, clearer, more meaningful experience. They are the currency of human contact."

—ROBERT MCKEE

"Fix" has several meanings. First, we're addicted to problem-solving. If someone tells us about an issue, we often go right to solving it (before actually listening to the complexity of the issue). To "fix" is also to set in stone, to provide a story that doesn't change.

When Tess was diagnosed with Asperger's, we presented it to her as simply a different kind of "operating system." And while it is one thing to say that, it is another to believe it when the world is telling you that your child is broken, and when there are so many challenges.

One morning, I came upon a drawing she had done in the kitchen, with this caption: "I LOVE EVERYTHING ABOUT ME!"

I had fixed her in a broken story, and she was telling a story of awesomeness.

Morning: Pay attention to the stories you tell about yourself and others today. Just notice them, without judgment.

Evening: What stories have you "fixed"? Which ones would you like to "un-fix?"

May 19

see them right now

"As long as you have certain desires about how it ought to be, you can't see how it is."

—RAM DASS

We live so much in the past or future, and so little in this moment.

My friend Susan Piver, in her book *The Wisdom of a Broken Heart*, tells the story of a breakdown she had after a love relationship ended. Sitting on the curb outside her house on trash day one week, sobbing, she suddenly realized that in that moment, her lover was not hurting her, that nothing was happening to her. That in that moment, she was okay and not suffering—that the hurt was in the past.

We drag so much forward with us, don't we? What if we let go of it on "trash day"?

Morning: "See them right now" is as true of seeing people in our lives right now as it is of seeing situations right now. What past can you give up today so you can see how things are right now?

Evening: What can you take to the curb?

May 20

"Cease striving. Then there will be transformation."

—CHUANG TSE

There is so much striving in the world.

We set the bar so high for ourselves. We lose sleep over it. We disconnect ourselves from our essential selves to reach the bar. We miss important moments in our family's lives to get there. Sometimes we even give up happiness in our pursuit of that bar.

And we rebel against the idea of lowering it.

Why? Is mediocrity really the opposite of striving? Is there no middle ground? Can we not give ourselves the grace to take a breath? What if we can only reach our goals by lowering our bar?

Morning: Reassess your goals today—see them as experiments rather than bars carved in stone. What happens when you change one of them to better reflect your priorities or your life in this moment?

Evening: What bars can you lower?

May 21

"You will recognize your own path when you come upon it, because you will suddenly have all the energy and imagination you will ever need."

—JERRY GILLIES

Imagine that you are a ball of light and that your job is to illuminate your own path.

To do that, you'll need to stop playing small. Let your light shine fully. And don't despair if you haven't found that path yet—the light you shine will help you navigate toward and through it.

Morning: How does it feel to be a ball of light, of energy, today?

Evening: What if your goal tomorrow was to keep that light from going out? How might you do that?

May 22

"It's a helluva start, being able to recognize what makes you happy."

—LUCILLE BALL

Do you trust your own heart to tell you what makes you happy? Or are you following a societal prescription for happiness?

My list includes feeling the cool sand under the hot surface of a beach. I really love that. And sitting quietly in the living room with my whole family there, reading. And showing up for people. All these things (and more) make me happy. They are simple things, as most happiness is.

Can you trust your own heart more to reveal what happiness is, rather than seeking it or trying to find it? It is not outside you. As Carl Jung has said, "Your vision will become clear only when you can look into your own heart. Who looks outside, dreams; who looks inside, awakes."

Morning: Make a list of what makes you happy. Add to it as you go through your day.

Evening: Read your list. Make space in your life for those things inside your own heart.

May 23

"The only journey is the journey within."

—RAINER MARIA RILKE

We don't allow for too much wandering. We have a destination, we plug in our departure and arrival addresses, and we get the most direct route to get us there, whether in driving, fitness, or personal exploration. We have given up the thrill of the side roads.

But it is the side roads where all the discoveries are—the little spots that give life its richness, like Frog and Teena's Fried Apple Pies that exist on no highway. What is the internal journey if not one of hidden spaces and unknown destinations? And yet we want to use our GPS and be efficient in that journey too.

No, we must wander.

Morning: Take side roads today when you travel. What is the internal equivalent of that for you? Is it allowing yourself to meditate or daydream or journal? How can you get off your internal highway and reduce your speed limit enough to see the landscape you are passing through?

Evening: What did you discover about your capacity to wander?

May 24

"Each time a person stands for an ideal, or acts to improve the lot of others, or strikes out against injustice, they send a tiny ripple of hope, and crossing each other from a million different centers of energy and daring, those ripples build a current which can sweep down the mightiest walls of oppression and resistance."

—ROBERT F. KENNEDY

I sat in a management meeting once and listened as the other vice presidents in the organization discussed whether an employee could post a flyer on the employee bulletin board about a "gay picnic." After some debate, in which I felt inadequate as an advocate for gay employees, one vice president said, to my shock, "Well, if someone put up a flyer for a 'KKK picnic,' we wouldn't allow that." At that, I sputtered.

I went to a class shortly afterward to learn how to be a better advocate for people who are GLBTQI. I knew I wanted to stand up for them, but felt inadequate to do so.

Morning: What are you standing up for?

Evening: What scares you about standing up for that? What information or resources would help you feel more confident in standing up for it?

May 25

*"Do not be daunted by the enormity of the world's grief.
Do justly, now. Love mercy, now. Walk humbly, now.
You are not obligated to complete the work,
but neither are you free to abandon it."*

—TALMUD

There is so much that needs doing. It can feel smothery and overwhelming.

We cannot do it all. But we can do something. And we must. Now.

Morning: Do what you can today. That's all you can do.

Evening: You are not free to abandon the work—what does that mean to you?

May 26

*"That's the good part of dying; when you've nothing
to lose, you run any risk you want."*

—RAY BRADBURY

The advice to live like you're dying is clichéd, really, but still
valid. Because you are. Dying.

Let us learn from those who are dying. Here are the top five
regrets of the dying, as recorded by a palliative nurse over many
years:

1. I wish I'd had the courage to live a life true to myself,
   not the life others expected of me.
2. I wish I hadn't worked so hard.
3. I wish I'd had the courage to express my feelings.
4. I wish I had stayed in touch with my friends.
5. I wish that I had let myself be happier.

Morning: Which of these resonates most deeply with you?
Which do you want to work on first?

Evening: What is your first step to not having these regrets?

May 27

"Happiness is within. It has nothing to do with how much applause you get or how many people praise you. Happiness comes when you believe that you have done something truly meaningful."

—MARTIN YAN

"Work that matters" is different for each one of us—and can only be defined by us for ourselves.

We cannot ascribe a hierarchy of "meaningfulness" to our work. Just because someone has a big title or paycheck or influence doesn't mean that their work is more meaningful than our own. Only we can know if we are doing work that matters.

Morning: Are you doing something truly meaningful? Pay attention today to the ways in which you are doing work that matters.

Evening: What did your attention to "work that matters" reveal to you today?

May 28

"Eat healthily, sleep well, breathe deeply, move harmoniously."

—JEAN-PIERRE BARRAL

Those four actions are simple, and yet they elude us, don't they?

We are bombarded with unhealthy food options, and increasingly more to do in our days and less time to sleep. Breathing deeply and moving harmoniously are often seen as luxuries, not necessities.

But imagine life if we did just these four practices. More energy, healthier bodies, well-rested lives full of relaxation and poise and flexibility.

Which one of these practices will you start with? Remember: Every action you take is either leading you toward or away from greater health and vitality. You choose.

Morning: Choose one of these practices and focus on it today. Notice what you notice about your energy levels as a result.

Evening: Incorporate this question in your days: With this choice, am I moving toward or away from greater health and vitality?

May 29

leave
some
things
undone.

"To learn which questions are unanswerable, and not to answer them: this skill is most needful in times of stress and darkness."

—URSULA K. LE GUIN

There is a fallacy that we can "have it all" and "do it all" and "know it all." We can't. And that's okay. Because some things need to be left un-had, undone, and unknown.

How does it feel to read that? Is it a relief? Or a source of anxiety? Your response to it might give you free data about yourself.

Morning: What can you leave undone today? Will you?

Evening: What can you let go of tomorrow? And the next day?

May 30

"Until you let someone in, you'll always be alone."

—CHASE ADAMS

My friend Nina let me in as she navigated Lou Gehrig's disease—in one blink, we went from polite lunches to me helping her onto the toilet when she could no longer walk. I was there for her when she died.

She knew she needed to let someone in—and that there was an awful and glorious vulnerability in that. I became her voice and her limbs and more. A stubborn, self-reliant woman, it was no doubt hard for her, but how much harder it would have been to navigate that illness alone—not just the physical illness but the emotional distress.

Nina let me in. And she taught me the value of letting people in, for which I will be forever grateful.

Morning: Do you let people in, or do you keep them at a distance, hiding the shadowy parts of yourself for fear of judgment? What are your patterns?

Evening: What, if you shared it, might be more bearable in your life? Can you? Will you?

Thomas Merton wrote that "there is always a temptation to diddle around in the contemplative life, making itsy-bitsy statues."

What happens when your participation in the contemplative life ranges far beyond making "itsy-bitsy statues?" When this daily practice is not just a hobby or a fad for you, but a way of life?

Our job is to embed and internalize this daily mindfulness into our lives. Structure is so important—things just don't happen without our attention to them.

Go beyond making "itsy-bitsy statues" this month.

June

"I name you today, heart fears. I am small, but you are smaller. You will not stop me. You have a voice, fears, and I must listen, but then I will open my heart. I will love you right to death."

—ANNA WHITE

To love someone else is an action that you control (even if it feels uncontrollable). And we do love control, don't we?

The greater action is not to love but to *allow yourself to be beloved.* This is the difference between seeing and being seen; one involves an action and the other requires an opening, a baring.

And it is "opening" that is most fearful. We are okay seeing; we are sometimes fearful of being seen. Our job is to practice that muscle and allow ourselves to be beloved.

Morning: It starts small. When you get a compliment, do you deflect it? "Oh, this old thing?" if someone compliments your sweater. Or, "I used to be way thinner," if someone says you're looking good. Allowing yourself to be beloved means, in part, opening yourself to the admiration of others. Can you simply say "thank you" the next time you get a compliment?

Evening: What is hard about being beloved for you?

June 1

"Humanity has advanced, when it has advanced, not because it has been sober, responsible, and cautious, but because it has been playful, rebellious, and immature."

—TOM ROBBINS

When children are small, some parents arrange "play dates," scheduled opportunities for kids to play with others. When we grow older, we forget to include play on our schedules in favor of being sober, responsible, and cautious.

More's the pity. We are weighted down with the separation we have devised between "work" and "play." There is great value in being playful, rebellious, and immature—reclaim that madness!

Morning: Ponder this today: If you could schedule any kind of play date, what would it be? What is keeping you from doing that?

Evening: What's a step toward playfulness that you could incorporate into your daily life, and how can you step toward that play date you pondered today?

June 2

"The world is full of magic things, patiently
waiting for our senses to grow sharper."

—W. B. YEATS

Our senses are wondrous avenues into the world, and yet they fall short, leaving a whole world that we cannot sense. That's what magic is, isn't it? That world beyond our senses?

We are tiny human engineers, trying to build scaffolds of sense and logic in our lives, disregarding the magic that lies between and beneath and behind all those structures we create. What happens in our lives when we simply let magic happen— without questioning it or scaling it or capturing it or measuring it? What happens when we let go of our need to engineer life?

Morning: Today, expect magic. See what happens.

Evening: What did you discover about magic today?

June 3

"The object isn't to make art, it's to be in that wonderful state which makes art inevitable."

—ROBERT HENRI

Making "art" seems scary to a lot of people. We respond with deflections—*I'm not creative,* or *I'm not an artist.*

But, as Henri said, the point is not the product—it is the process, the openness and willingness we create in our days to see life itself as a work of art. And that work of art we call life comes in many forms—for some, it is parenting. For others, it is being in nature. For still others, it is managing a company. Each has an artfulness to be respected and honored. Each requires a spirit of creation rather than of inevitability or mandate.

Morning: In what ways can you cultivate a spirit of artfulness in your life today?

Evening: How can you continue to bridge the gap between life and art?

"Stop seeking out the storms and enjoy more fully the sunlight."

—GORDON B. HINCKLEY

Sure, the storms are there. Life can be difficult, the skies are sometimes dark and menacing, and things go "wrong," or seem to. And we can always find storms if we look for them.

What if, instead, we dedicated ourselves to finding the sunlight? To nurturing the growth that happens when the sky is bright blue?

What if we enjoyed the sunlight without looking to the horizon for the next dark cloud? Or saw the clouds in a different way?

Morning: Enjoy the "sunlight" today, in whatever way makes you happy.

Evening: Think about your patterns—do you ever fully let yourself enjoy life, or are you waiting for the other shoe to drop, assuming that darkness will follow? How might altering that pattern give you more joy? How might seeing darkness differently change things for you?

June 5

"We are all broken and wounded in this world. Some choose to grow strong at the broken places."

—HAROLD J. DUARTE-BERNHARDT

We know that beautiful things are beautiful. By definition (even though our definitions of beauty might differ—and likely do.)

But what we might not recognize is that difficult things, and awkward and broken things, and devastating and awful things, also have a beauty.

As Vance Havner has written, "God uses broken things. It takes broken soil to produce a crop, broken clouds to give rain, broken grain to give bread, broken bread to give strength. It is the broken alabaster box that gives forth perfume. It is Peter, weeping bitterly, who returns to greater power than ever."

The bigger job we have is in finding the beauty in those things.

Morning: Look for beauty in brokenness. It is there. Imagine your own "scars" as traced with gold.

Evening: What beauty did you find today?

June 6

"What I suddenly understood was that a thank-you note isn't the price you pay for receiving a gift, as so many children think it is, a kind of minimum tribute or toll, but an opportunity to count your blessings. And gratitude isn't what you give in exchange for something; it's what you feel when you are blessed—blessed to have family and friends who care about you, and who want to see you happy. Hence the joy from thanking."

—WILL SCHWALBE

In 2009, I started writing a thank-you note every morning. I still do it. Some are mailed and some are not. I read the news and when I see good being done, I write a note to the person who has reached beyond him or herself to bring light to the world. It has informed what I look for in the world—not evil, but evidence of good.

Writing a thank-you note is a daily practice of counting my blessings, and they are many, even when it feels like things are broken.

Morning: To whom can you write a thank-you note today? Write it.

Evening: Did you find yourself looking for things to be thankful for tomorrow? If not, can you?

June 7

"The ultimate of being successful is the luxury of giving yourself the time to do what you want to do."

—LEONTYNE PRICE

It is easier to say what we don't want than to say what we do want, isn't it? For many of us, that is true. If it is true for you, your goal today is to brainstorm (without any judgment) this list: "What I want to do."

Once you've got that started, think about how you can create space in your busy life to take a step forward into that list. Sometimes, often, that requires letting something(s) go.

Morning: Work on your list today—what do you most want to do?

Evening: Now list the things that stand in the way of that list. What will you let go of?

June 8

"Simple can be harder than complex: You have to work hard to get your thinking clean to make it simple. But it's worth it in the end because once you get there, you can move mountains."

—STEVE JOBS

Is your thinking clean?

You will immediately know the answer to that question: Yes or No.

If yes, carry on. If no, consider what might be muddying your thinking—is it exhaustion, an addiction to sugar, too many things that have to happen at once, fear, self-doubt, overwork?

Morning: Make a list of what is muddying your thinking. Pay attention to moments in the day when you feel clarity, and moments when you don't. When things feel simple, and complicated. Take notes.

Evening: Review your notes—what patterns can you discern? What causes can you identify for muddy, complicated thinking? What is the path toward more simplicity and clearer thinking?

June 9

"Just this once, let it be easy."

—CYNTHIA LORD

I used to work with a man who made his training models and exercises so complicated that his clients would always need him around to explain things—he built into the process a requirement for his services.

My process has always been the polar opposite of that—make it as easy as possible for people to integrate the learning into their own toolbox so it can serve them when I'm not there.

We didn't work together for very long.

I find that the greatest learnings in our lives are very simple. Big and complex, perhaps, but not complicated.

And I find that we are a wee bit addicted to things that aren't easy—as if "complicated" is a badge of honor. Today, let it be easy.

Morning: Today, what in your life can you find that really is simple but has been made complicated? Focus on ferreting these complications out.

Evening: Make this your mantra for tomorrow: "Just this once, let it be easy." There is no shame in easy; there is great beauty in it.

June 10

A simple formula: Showing up (being present) is better than any present.

Morning: Today, show up for someone else.

Evening: Giving of ourselves often takes more time and energy than just pressing a button on the computer to donate money or support a cause with cash. Both are important. In what ways can you give of yourself this week?

June 11

"Until we can receive with an open heart, we're never really giving with an open heart. When we attach judgment to receiving help, we knowingly or unknowingly attach judgment to giving help."

—BRENÉ BROWN

How we give is how we receive, as Brené Brown has said. If we want to be able to give wholeheartedly, we have to learn to receive wholeheartedly, with none of the shame sometimes associated with receiving help.

Giving and receiving seem so simple, but they are not. We complicate them with our stories of what it means to need help, don't we? We equate being able to help with power; and needing help with vulnerability and less-than. We find it hard to receive help because we are stuck in a model of reciprocity—if I receive, I must repay. Perhaps that model doesn't serve us well.

Morning: Today, focus on how you feel about giving and receiving help. Which is easier for you? Do you place any judgment on the person needing your help? Or on yourself, if you're the person in need?

Evening: Keep noticing what you notice (without judgment—it's just good information for you) about giving and receiving.

June 12

"How would your life be different if . . . You stopped making negative judgmental assumptions about people you encounter? Let today be the day . . . You look for the good in everyone you meet and respect their journey."

—STEVE MARABOLI

Respecting the journeys of others is one way to become someone you respect. Consider this radical idea: Stop judging the people you encounter and extend to them the kind of respect you would like to have extended to yourself. That's the first step.

Morning: At lunchtime every day, pause and ask yourself this question: Am I becoming someone I respect?

Evening: What attributes do you respect in other people? Which of those attributes would you like to develop? Start with one. Respect is built by consistency over time.

June 13

"Honesty is more than not lying. It is truth telling, truth speaking, truth living, and truth loving."

—JAMES E. FAUST

Integrity is a verb, a series of actions, not just the absence of untruth.

Are you truth telling?
Are you truth speaking?
Are you truth living?
Are you truth loving?

Morning: Think about these four questions today. In the moment, ask them and simply sit with your response, without judging yourself.

Evening: Did you discover anything about integrity in these four questions?

June 14

"The word 'listen' contains the same letters as the word 'silent.'"

—ALFRED BRENDEL

We are attuned to the world outside ourselves. When the garbage truck turns the corner, we panic, realizing we have forgotten to put the trash out. We run to get to the curb before the truck does.

When the wind makes a certain sound in the trees, we know it will soon rain.

There is so much we know (and don't know) by listening to the world.

But are we ever silent enough to listen to ourselves? What signals are we missing because our world is so noisy? What is our life telling us but we are not hearing?

Morning: Incorporate just five minutes of absolute silence into your day today. See what happens.

Evening: You know more than you think you know. Listen to yourself.

June 15

"Intuition is seeing with the soul."

—DEAN KOONTZ

There is something deeper than reason or measurement or external validity. You know it—you have felt it. The word "intuition" comes from the Latin *intueri*, which translates as "to look inside."

We are surrounded by intuition all the time—and yet we dismiss our intuition because we can't "prove" it. At a leadership conference years ago, we were asked which of a set of objects would help us survive in the wilderness. I quietly offered my suggestion. "What's the evidence to support that?" someone asked. "I don't know—I just feel it's important." My idea was dismissed for lack of evidence and I didn't follow up on it, because I discounted my own intuition and didn't have empirical language to back up my claim.

When the answers were revealed, my suggestion was at the top of the list. Here's to loosening our grip on the need to prove, measure, and solve. There is a whole world beyond those constraints.

Morning: Notice when you feel you are "seeing with your soul." How does that feel? How do you know what your intuition is telling you? How often do you discount it?

Evening: How often do you demand "evidence" from others?

June 16

"The most important distinction anyone can ever make in their life is between who they are as an individual and their connection with others."

ANNÉ LINDEN

A lack of boundaries invites a lack of respect, plain and simple. If we can't set boundaries for ourselves, we cannot blame others for imposing on us—they can't know if we don't know where we end and they begin.

Even children need clear boundaries—they need to know where they start and stop, and where you start and stop. They need clarity on what works and what doesn't. So do adults. We need practice on discerning what works for us and what doesn't, on what we will tolerate and what we will not. Our job is to make that clear to others and seek that information from them as well.

Morning: Today, notice the people and places that tend to drain you. These are probably great places to start creating clear boundaries for yourself.

Evening: The words "yes" and "no" can correlate to boundary setting—how addicted are you to the word "yes" and why? Are you a people pleaser who "hates to let people down"? Tomorrow, practice setting boundaries with the word "no."

June 17

"What one does is what counts. Not what one had the intention of doing."

—PABLO PICASSO

Don't carry around with you the art you intended to make, the childhood you wanted to create for your kids, the book you meant to write. Purge those undone things from your portfolio. No need for excuses, now, for the undone or half done or done poorly. You can learn from them, but then purge them.

Rather, put out into the world the portfolio of what you have done well, accomplished, created. Let it speak for you—no need for excuses or deflections. No "it could have been better," or "this is what I wanted to create." Just "here is my work in the world."

Morning: Notice how many times today you feel the need to deflect attention from your work.

Evening: What do you want/need to purge from your portfolio? What is extra weight that you feel you have to make excuses for? Take it out.

June 18

"Life is the dancer and you are the dance."

—ECKHART TOLLE

In other words, dance. Move.

Many of us have lost the freedom to move we once had as a child. Even if you feel you must be alone when you dance, do it anyway. Reconnect your head to your body—it will take some practice if there has been a big disconnect for a long time.

There is evidence that dancing has great health benefits. Map your way into a healthier landscape with your dance, your movement, the way your body responds to fear, fight, love, freedom. Dance to them all and discover the terrain of your own body.

Morning: Put on some music (start with Pharrell's "Happy") and dance for five minutes to start your day. How did that feel?

Evening: How can you incorporate dance into your day?

"The best day of your life is the one on which you decide your life is your own. No apologies or excuses. No one to lean on, rely on, or blame. The gift is yours—it is an amazing journey—and you alone are responsible for the quality of it. This is the day your life really begins."

—BOB MOAWAD

As many have said, friends don't need your excuses and enemies won't believe them anyway. So why make them? What does taking full responsibility for our lives look like in practice?

Morning: Today, when you find yourself making an excuse, stop yourself. Excuses help us abdicate personal responsibility— own the responsibility instead.

Evening: What discoveries did you make today? Often we realize we are more prone to making excuses than we thought. To whom or to what are you shifting blame? How does it feel to take that on yourself instead?

"Being still does not mean don't move. It means move in peace."

—E'YEN A. GARDNER

People are forever telling us to be still. Don't they understand that we rarely have time for immobility? What if we redefine stillness as E'yen Gardner has done: Moving in peace.

Are you moving in peace? Or do you feel torn in a thousand directions? Are you moving in fear or anticipation or regret in your life? What is the jet propulsion of your movement through life? Anger? Love? War? Peace?

Morning: I love this definition of being still. Today, focus on "moving in peace." Notice how your body interprets that action.

Evening: When you focused on "moving in peace" as your definition of stillness, how did that change the way you moved through the world today?

June 21

"As soon as you trust yourself, you will know how to live."

—JOHANN WOLFGANG VON GOETHE

Is self-trust something we can learn? It is, according to Cynthia Wall, author of *The Courage to Trust*. She suggests these three steps:

Eliminate people from your life who imbue your life with self-doubt. Who are these people in your life?

Keep promises to yourself. You can't trust yourself if you are not trustworthy.

Speak to yourself with kindness. When you hear negative self messages, short-circuit them with a more understanding message.

Morning: Today, practice the three steps above and ask yourself these questions to get to the heart of them: Who leaves you questioning yourself rather than believing in yourself? What promises to yourself can you actively keep today? What are the messages you are speaking to yourself? Are they kindly?

Evening: Which step was the hardest for you? Work on that one tomorrow, and beyond.

June 22

"And so taking the long way home through the market I slow my pace down. It doesn't come naturally. My legs are programmed to trot briskly and my arms to pump up and down like pistons, but I force myself to stroll past the stalls and pavement cafes. To enjoy just being somewhere, rather than rushing from somewhere, to somewhere. Inhaling deep lungfuls of air, instead of my usual shallow breaths. I take a moment to just stop and look around me. And smile to myself. For the first time in a long time, I can, quite literally, smell the coffee."

—ALEXANDRA POTTER

Are you busy? Will your life slow down or get faster? Are you using the pace of your life as a status symbol: I'm so in demand, I have so much to do, I fly so much, I have a full plate.

Sometimes the action we need to take is counterintuitive to what we believe the situation calls for. Sometimes the pace of our lives calls for opting out.

What happens when you slow down? Find out.

Morning: Today, when life feels crazed and too busy, take three deep breaths and say this to yourself: "Everything needs a chance to unfold, and unfolding requires time. Slow down, and then slow down some more."

Evening: What did you notice about your resistance to or embrace of slowing down?

June 23

"The roots of all goodness lie in the soil of appreciation for goodness."

—DALAI LAMA

There is goodness all around us, hidden amidst news reports that focus on the dire and despairing. If we can build our muscle of appreciating and celebrating goodness, we can grow even more goodness.

With which do you surround yourself—goodness or evil?

Morning: With every post on Facebook or on your blog, ask yourself this question: What is the quality of my engagement with the world in posting this? Positive or negative?

Evening: How does it feel to ask the question about the quality of energy you are putting into the world? Did you notice that it had an impact on your choices today?

June 24

"Some people drink from the fountain of knowledge; others just gargle."

—ROBERT ANTHONY

Hydrate yourself today—whether with a drink from the fountain of knowledge or from your stainless steel water bottle. Don't just gargle—drink deeply. Your mind and body are thirsty—so thirsty.

Morning: Fill a water bottle as you start your day. Drink it by lunchtime. Fill it again and drink it by dinnertime. Repeat daily. Water carries goodness.

Evening: Do you miss drinking from the fountain of knowledge? Do you love when someone sparks that urge? Follow the path back to that kind of brain hydration.

June 25

"I'm here. I love you. I don't care if you need to stay up crying all night long, I will stay with you. There's nothing you can ever do to lose my love. I will protect you until you die, and after your death I will still protect you. I am stronger than Depression and I am braver than Loneliness and nothing will ever exhaust me."

—ELIZABETH GILBERT

Poet Andrea Gibson has started a movement called Stay Here with Me, focused on creating a space where people who are suicidal can share their stories and, hopefully, be inspired to stay here with us.

How much we all need that message—you're important to me, I love you, I am here for you, you matter.

Morning: Who are your "human survival units" that provide the kind of consistency of which Elizabeth Gilbert writes?

Evening: For whom are you a human survival unit? When's the last time you connected with that person? Reconnect.

June 26

"The remarkable thing is that it is the crowded life that is most easily remembered. A life full of turns, achievements, disappointments, surprises and crises is a life full of landmarks. The empty life has even its few details blurred, and cannot be remembered with certainty."

—ERIC HOFFER

We all need landmarks. Things to orient by.

I remember when John Kennedy Jr. died in a plane crash, becoming disoriented about what was up and down in a white-out, unable to gauge where he was. It happened to me driving up Old Fort Mountain a few years later: fog, dense and swirling in my headlights. Where was road and where was sky? I needed landmarks to make sense of it.

So, too, with life. What are you orienting by?

Morning: Pay attention to physical landmarks today. What landmarks do you rely on as you walk or drive around your town today? Bring your landmarks to the level of conscious awareness of them.

Evening: What are the key landmarks of your life's journey thus far? Make a list. What would you like to add to that list?

June 27

"It was . . . disconcerting to examine your charts before a proposed flight only to find that in many cases the bulk of the terrain over which you had to fly was bluntly marked: 'UNSURVEYED.' It was as if the mapmakers had said, 'We are aware that between this spot and that one, there are several hundred thousands of acres, but until you make a forced landing there, we won't know whether it is mud, desert, or jungle—and the chances are we won't know then!'"

—BERYL MARKHAM

Imagine your heart is unsurveyed territory. You can't know what is there unless you make a forced landing there. Once you do, you can know the topography of that place—what is in your heart? What peaks, what valleys? What mud pits? What jungles? Does the sun shine brightly in that land, or not?

Morning: Imagine your heart is an unmarked terrain. Land there, and map what you find.

Evening: As you go through your days, add to your heart map. Explore it. Map it.

June 28

"In wisdom gathered over time I have found that every experience is a form of exploration."

—ANSEL ADAMS

Imagine every morning that you are an explorer. What do explorers do? They watch, see, pay attention closely. They push against boundaries of what is known into what is unknown. They map their way into uncharted waters; they seek context from seen to unseen.

Explorers take risks. They seek. They travel lightly to remain agile. They see exploration in the everyday. They are curious.

Morning: If you are a true explorer today, how does that change the way you engage with the world?

Evening: How did being an explorer in this day inform the days to come?

June 29

"You have not lived today until you have done something for someone who can never repay you."

—JOHN BUNYAN

It is easy to think that others will help. That someone more qualified will stop and pay attention and offer assistance. That someone with more resources will surely step up.

But a real hero is the person who does what she can for someone who can never repay her.

What stops you from offering a hand? From doing what you can? Fear of too much involvement? Rejection? Feeling that you can't do enough, that your resources are limited?

Offer a hand anyway. Imagine it not as a reciprocal relationship but as handing one another along, passing the baton.

Morning: Today, look for opportunities to help someone else. Then help them.

Evening: How did it feel to be a helper, to offer your hand without expectation of repayment?

June 30

You are only responsible for your own actions—as much as you might like to control the actions of others, you cannot. This is both freeing and horrifying, of course.

How you spend your days is how you spend your life. If you are moving away from a daily practice of mindfulness, and this book is sitting idly by your bed, there is no one who can make that right but you. Not me, the author, or a friend who notices you've stopped. Just you.

July

"Never be afraid to raise your voice for honesty and truth and compassion against injustice and lying and greed. If people all over the world . . . would do this, it would change the earth."

—WILLIAM FAULKNER

I am an advocate for kids with autism because I have one of my own. I am also an advocate for people who share nothing in common with me because it is the right thing to do. Can we extend our advocacy beyond the limits of our own human experience?

For what or for whom are you an advocate?

Morning: Today, speak up for honesty and truth and compassion outside your own sphere. Extend yourself to speak out against injustices you yourself will never experience.

Evening: What are the costs of speaking up? What are the costs of not speaking up?

*"People often say that this or that person has not yet found himself.
But the self is not something one finds, it is something one creates."*

—THOMAS SZASZ

When I went to college, I kept looking around for the loud-
speakers that would tell me things, like the loudspeaker in high
school that told us when to go to lunch, or what was next, or
which clubs we could choose. Imagine my surprise when I realized there wasn't one—that it was up to me to seek out the information I needed, that no one would tell me what my options
were, that I was, in fact, an active participant in the shaping of
my life.

Every day, we are creating the story of our lives—by the
choices we live, by the stories we tell, by the "yes" and the "no"
of our moments, and by the ways in which we actively create our
lives, or don't.

Morning: What loudspeaker are you waiting to find? One that
gives permission? Imagine yourself as that loudspeaker today—
you are the one who gives permission.

Evening: What are you waiting for?

July 2

*"I thought I could describe a state; make a map of sorrow.
Sorrow, however, turns out to be not a state but a process."*

—C. S. LEWIS

I grew up in a neighborhood surrounded by woods and streams, in a day in which kids went out in the morning, played all day, and came home when their fathers whistled to let them know it was dinnertime, each father's whistle distinct from the others. We spent many Saturdays damming up the creek, watching it grow higher, seeing it stagnate, and then explode over or through the dam. Such power.

Most things in life are not static states—if they are, we don't stay there long. Life is a flow, instead. Our challenges arise when we try to dam the flow, keep things the same, hold on to a moment in time that is fleeting, make concrete something that is fluid.

Morning: What loss in your life have you dammed up? Can you let it flow into the next pool of your life? Can you let the river flow and see it as a process, not a static place?

Evening: Life is all process, not product. It isn't the end, it's the getting there. What can you let go of?

July 3

"A map does not just chart, it unlocks and formulates meaning; it forms bridges between here and there, between disparate ideas that we did not know were previously connected."

—REIF LARSEN

I am enamored with maps. Why? I'm not entirely sure. Perhaps it is the way we see that which matters to us when we map it—just as we can tell what is important to us by what we photograph. Maybe it is because maps are a process of learning where we have been and where we are going.

In thinking about the events of my life, I usually map them before writing about them—the visualization of how I map them tells me things. When I draw the losses in my life as caverns, there is knowing there. When I draw the births of my daughters as clouds, I am telling myself something. Just as language unlocks meaning, so do the maps of our lives.

Morning: Draw a simple map today—the map of how you get to work, or school, or to the grocery store. See what you discover by mapping. What is big and what is little on your map? What is and isn't included?

Evening: Draw a map each day for a week. Pick a topic: the map of your loves, your depressions, your path to where you are today. Notice what you discover.

July 4

"Grief can be a burden, but also an anchor. You get used to the weight, how it holds you in place."

—SARAH DESSEN

I fall into darkness sometimes. Do you?

And then sometimes I feel I might float away. Do you ever feel that way? Like I am a cloud, unhooked from the earth. Maybe it is wishful thinking—what freedom to soar.

Somewhere between those two places, up there and down below in a black cave, is where I live. I feel such euphoria sometimes, and such grief at others. I imagine we all do—perhaps this is the human condition. Where we find solace, perhaps, is in reframing each of those states—perhaps that black cave of loss is our anchor, keeping us from floating away so we can stay in this world.

When I go to the dentist, I have learned to ask for the weighted vest they use for X-rays as my comfort. Perhaps our grief can serve the same purpose.

Morning: As you feel darkness today, reframe it as your anchor, your comfort, rather than your enemy.

Evening: What grief can you reframe as your anchor?

July 5

"We are in community each time we find a place where we belong."

—PETER F. BLOCK

There is a difference between loneliness and solitude. Solitude is necessary at times—to be alone, and to learn how to be alone with ourselves, is essential in our lives. But loneliness is something different—it is a place of craving, of unsettledness, of lack rather than wholeness.

Community is an intention, not a circumstance—just as life is a verb, community is an active and not a passive verb.

Morning: Are you lonely? What step toward community can you make today?

Evening: What communities are you in that sustain and buoy you? What communities drain you? Which can you let go of? Which can you strengthen?

July 6

"In a flash of wonderment she saw firm, continuous ground under her feet, stretching from back then to right now and on and on as far as her eyes could take her."

—ANN BRASHARES

When I lived in Washington, DC, we used to sit on the apartment roof so I could imagine how to navigate the city. It was hard for me, having always lived in small, Southern towns where NE and SW didn't exist in daily discussions. My friends tried to orient me. "Imagine a central point," they would say, "with four quadrants spreading out from that spot." Intellectually, I got it. Sitting on the roof helped. But when I got into a traffic-circle swirl, all was lost. How can we orient ourselves in the reality of circumstance, rather than in the idea of four neat quadrants?

Where are you standing telling your story? Perhaps that is the "central point" of which my friends spoke. Describe the ground of your life—is it hospitable? Is it desert? Is it lush? Imagine the horizon—is it a fixed line or one you can imagine moving as you walk toward it? Where does the sun rise and set?

Morning: Imagine four quadrants spreading out from each spot you inhabit today. What is in each of those quadrants? How does it feel to orient yourself in this way?

Evening: Feel the ground under your feet in this way every day. Know where you are.

July 7

create
your
own
atlas

"What wouldn't I give now for a never-changing map of the ever-constant ineffable? To possess, as it were, an atlas of clouds."

—DAVID MITCHELL

"Did you see the man in the moon?" I asked my host family in Sri Lanka. I was there as a sixteen-year-old exchange student. They looked at me like I was crazy. "What?" my host sister, Nilanthi, asked. "We see a rabbit in the moon," she explained. We each pointed to the moon—what I saw as eyes, she saw as ears.

In such a way, we create our own atlas of the world around us. Influenced by culture, of course, and by our own way of being in the world—what we believe and don't believe, what we care about and don't.

The moon waxes and wanes; the man and rabbit go away and come back again, just like the "cloud bones" that Tess used to see in the sky. There is a physicality to what is inexpressible and ineffable in our lives—creating an atlas helps us see what we feel. Is it a man in the moon or a rabbit? Explore.

Morning: Map what love looks like. Map what heartbreak looks like. If they are cloud forms, what are those shapes?

Evening: Describe the ineffable in terms of edges or shapes this week—see what you uncover.

July 8

"*Everyone thinks of changing the world, but
no one thinks of changing himself.*"

—LEO TOLSTOY

What we resist looms larger, grows in importance and potency.
Resisting change makes its effect even greater in our lives—it
becomes more powerful the more we push against it. That's just
how it works.

When we think about change, many times we think about
the world changing outside ourselves. Things we love may go
away, our fortunes may disappear, our health may falter. These
are external changes that we can either resist or walk with, hand
in hand. What Tolstoy is reminding us is that we have infinite
capacity to change ourselves—to embrace internal changes and
explore them first.

Morning: What would you like to change about yourself? What
is holding you down or back? What can you practice daily in
order to make that change?

Evening: In a year, how would you like your vast, rich, internal
life to be different? How will you get there?

July 9

don't fill the gaps, explore them.

"Take that one thing you don't like about yourself and more often than not that's the one thing that makes you more special. Whether it's that gap in your teeth, or that mole you never liked, or your skin color."

—SHAY MITCHELL

We aspire so much to unrealistic ideals, don't we? Perfect teeth, tiny hips, luscious skin. And because of those aspirations, we find a gap between what is and what we believe would make us happier, more desirable, name your goal. This gap is unhealthy and damaging, and yet we try so hard to bridge that gap rather than be content with who we are.

What happens if we step back from that gap and explore the need that informs it?

Morning: Make a list of things you don't like about yourself. Reframe each one as something that makes you special. If this is difficult, imagine how your friends might describe you using that list of things you've outlined.

Evening: Choose one of the things on your list. Accentuate it. Explore it fully. Own it.

July 10

"Today I choose life. Every morning when I wake up I can choose joy, happiness, negativity, pain. . . . To feel the freedom that comes from being able to continue to make mistakes and choices—today I choose to feel life, not to deny my humanity but embrace it."

—KEVYN AUCOIN

I heard someone once say "I've decided to be happy in advance," and I've lived by that approach ever since, knowing I have a choice to choose happy, or not.

What are the patterns of how I define life? As full of possibility, as full of joy and relationship and a light that I can know because I also know great darkness. What she chooses is always dark, blame, woe, hardship, and joylessness.

We are choosing daily. Not by ignoring circumstances that are hateful or hard, but by embracing them as part of life, not as all of life.

Morning: Choose joy and happiness today. See what happens.

Evening: Know each morning that you are completely in charge, not of your circumstance always, but of how you are in that circumstance. Choose life.

July 11

"Set patterns, incapable of adaptability, of pliability, only offer a better cage. Truth is outside of all patterns."

—BRUCE LEE

How do we imprison ourselves by assuming the cage is real and the door is locked?

The cage in which we find ourselves—big or small, luxurious or harsh—is built by the strong patterns we embed into our lives. It can easily be opened by a simple mindfulness about those patterns, and about which serve us and which imprison us.

Open the door.

Morning: What patterns do you fall into when you visit your family? Do you play small? Do you seek confrontation? Do you become quiet? Think about visits home (or your equivalent). Make a list of the patterns you adopt.

Evening: Can you see those patterns as a cage, holding you in stasis with this group of people? Would a more honest relationship be built around how you have all evolved? How might you break one of those patterns?

July 12

"Everything is an experiment."

—TIBOR KALMAN

When I teach writing, I always teach that our focus is the process and not the product. It is never easy for students to fully grasp that because most of us are raised in cultures that emphasize outcome, deliverables, product.

Writer Natalie Goldberg has written, "Practice is something you choose to do on a regular basis with no vision of an outcome; the aim is not improvement, not getting somewhere. You do it because you do it. You show up whether you want to or not. . . . This continual practice expresses your true determination, signals to your unconscious, to your deep resistance that you mean business." She writes further, "What practice builds in us is a true confidence that can't be derived from outward signs of success—fame, money, beauty. This confidence comes from the fact that you show up over and over again. That you do what you say you are going to do."

Morning: Imagine that everything you are doing today is an experiment and that your job is simply to show up whether you want to or not.

Evening: How does it feel to focus on showing up rather than the product you create? On seeing life itself as an experiment?

July 13

"Each of us has his own rhythm of suffering."

—ROLAND BARTHES

We all feel loss in our lives. And for each of us, it will have a different tempo and rhythm. Some days, a quickening like a panic attack. Other days, the slow lumbering movement of manatees in warm water.

We can only feel what we feel, at whatever tempo it shows up for us. Don't hurry grief—you don't need to feel better for anyone else. Can you let yourself move to the rhythm of your own heart today? Is it broken? What rhythm is that?

Morning: Let go of external expectations of how quickly or slowly you move through the loss you feel today. Imagine your heart informing how you move today. What does that look like?

Evening: Who tries to hurry you through the hard places? Or are you hurrying yourself to spare the feelings of others? What happens when you linger there so you don't miss the lessons of grief?

July 14

"Nothing is a waste of time if you use the experience wisely."

—AUGUSTE RODIN

Someone once asked if I felt my first marriage was a waste of time. I was shocked not so much by the question but by the very idea that any time I had lived and learned through could be a waste of time.

I'm glad I was shocked—I still would be. Not only does that worldview negate huge chunks of our lives, potentially, but it also focuses only on product, not process. Did I learn a lot in those seven years? A tremendous amount that helped shape who I am today. Could that ever be seen as a waste?

Process, not product. Learning, not winning.

Morning: Tess loves to watch reruns of *Beakman's World*, a science show for kids, in which the main character is well known for saying "Everything goes somewhere!" Imagine a day without waste today, everything going somewhere. How does that change things?

Evening: Are you more process or product oriented? If you are product (outcome) focused, consider this possibility: Product is improved in direct relationship to the quality of our engagement with the process.

July 15

*"When I fully enter time's swift current, enter into the
current moment with the weight of all my attention, I
slow the torrent with the weight of me all here."*

—ANN VOSKAMP

Once when walking up Capitol Hill in DC with a friend, I got a
little irritated because he was walking so slowly. Always ahead by
a few steps, I kept my head down and focused on getting to the
top of a long incline. And still, he stayed behind. When I got
to the top, I turned to watch him. Finally, he stood beside me.

"Weren't those cherry blossoms amazing?" he asked.

"What cherry blossoms?" I replied.

Morning: What keeps you from being here now? What are
you racing toward that is obscuring your view of the cherry
blossoms?

Evening: Do you have a hard time being in this moment? Take
three deep breaths when you feel yourself racing forward, and
with each inhale, say, "Hello, moment." With each exhale, say,
"I am here." You will be asked to do this activity several times
in this book because it is such a simple, grounding response to
life.

July 16

". . . there are shadows because there are hills."

—E. M. FORSTER

Sometimes when I feel panicky and like I need to escape, I ask myself a simple question: "What are you running from?" (Sometimes, often, that question is easier to answer than "What are you running toward?")

It takes spirit to stay, to resist running away. It takes spirit to sit and embrace your shadow—there is a dark side to us all, after all. What would happen if we didn't run from it?

Morning: Don't race your own shadow today. Let it fill you up instead. Let yourself burst with shadow.

Evening: What are you running from?

July 17

"And once the storm is over, you won't remember how you made it through, how you managed to survive. You won't even be sure, whether the storm is really over. But one thing is certain. When you come out of the storm, you won't be the same person who walked in. That's what this storm's all about."

—HARUKI MURAKAMI

Annealing is a heat process whereby a metal is heated to a specific temperature and then allowed to cool slowly. This softens the metal, which means it can be cut and shaped more easily.

Fire. Storm. Darkness. Pestilence. Loss.

Let yourself be transformed by walking into the heat, made soft by its fire.

Morning: Imagine going on a journey where you come back a different person, transformed in some significant way. Is this fearful or exciting to you?

Evening: What are the storms in your life? Can you get to the eye of those storms and survive?

July 18

"If you desire healing,
let yourself fall ill
let yourself fall ill."

—RUMI

We can't learn from what we deny.
 We can't be healed if we can't allow that we are ill.
 We can't win what we're not willing to lose.
 We can't deny what it is we need to learn.
 What are you denying?

Morning: Make a list of what you have denied in the past. Is there a pattern in that list? What can you learn from that pattern?

Evening: Are you willing to fall ill in order to heal?

July 19

"Don't let the fear of striking out hold you back."

—BABE RUTH

When did you stop going to bat for fearing of striking out? We all do it at some point—when did you? That question could easily be, when did you stop being a poet, an artist, a leader, a joy-filled stick of dynamite?

Professional athletes watch training films of themselves to learn how and why they struck out—can you pay that kind of attention to your life without flinching? Can you pay attention in that way without resorting to blaming or excuses—just to learn, instead?

Morning: Pay attention today as if you were filming a training film of yourself—what patterns can you find? What actions do you take when you're questioned, when you're praised, when you drop the ball, and when you catch it? Look for answers, not wins.

Evening: What did you learn about your patterns today? Were you able to observe them without judging yourself for having those patterns? Remember: We can judge or we can learn, but we can't do both at the same time—choose learning.

July 20

don't polish
the jagged
edges.

*"A writer's heart, a poet's heart, an artist's heart, a
musician's heart is always breaking. It is through that
broken window that we see the world . . ."*

—ALICE WALKER

Neat and tidy. That's how we like our movies and our novels,
but those clean-edged moments lack surface tension; there is
nothing for us to hold onto after watching or reading them.
What if we focused on enough jaggedness in our lives to form
toeholds and handholds, something to grab onto instead of
slickness and ice?

Morning: Make a list of the broken things you encounter
today—clouds, grain, friendships, love—be an explorer of jaggedness and note what you find.

Evening: What beauty do you find in that list? Break something
open tomorrow, on purpose.

July 21

"One is never afraid of the unknown; one is
afraid of the known coming to an end."

—JIDDU KRISHNAMURTI

Wow.

Do you ever read a quote and think to yourself, "Yes! This is exactly it!"

That's what this quote from Krishnamurti does to me—we don't fear what we don't know; we fear the end of what we do know.

In college, I lived in a house with friends one year, and there was a couple that lived in the basement. We heard furniture moving down there one day, but then screams, and we realized in an instant that those weren't furniture sounds, but the sounds of the woman being thrown against the wall by her boyfriend. We rushed down; he left.

And yet, when he came back later that night, she let him in—my first recognition of the fear we have of the known coming to an end, regardless of the quality of the known.

Morning: What are you afraid will end? How does that keep you from leaning into the unknown?

Evening: Create a "what if" list. What if this relationship ended? What if I needed to move? What if . . . Create as complete a list as you can. Notice what you notice about the writing of it, and your reaction to it once written.

July 22

"Nothing is, unless our thinking makes it so."

—WILLIAM SHAKESPEARE

One of my earliest epiphanies came with my first airplane ride at age sixteen. Suddenly, as we took off, people got very tiny. My school was invisible very quickly. Whether or not Greg Alexander invited me to the prom was—*poof*—gone. I was unprepared and completely open to this massive change of perspective. My mind raced with the ramifications of it—nothing matters, I thought. And yet, at the end of that journey, we had to land again, and people became large again and things mattered again, but never in the same way.

Perspective is worth 80 IQ points, someone has said. At least, I would add.

Morning: How can you change your perspective today, as I did in that plane? What movement will give you a different vantage point on "what is"?

Evening: If I hold a large ball that is half red and half white, and you see only the white side, and I see only the red side, guess what we each will answer when asked what color that ball is. Get in the habit of asking yourself this question: "What else might be true?"

July 23

"The best way to treat obstacles is to use them as stepping-stones. Laugh at them, tread on them, and let them lead you to something better."

—ENID BLYTON

We don't pay much attention to our verbs, but we should. When a woman in a creativity retreat talked about "puking up eighty pages of her novel," we played with what the use of the verb "to puke" revealed about how she felt about writing. Turns out, she discovered she is a visual artist instead.

When corporations fill their vision statements with "We will study" or "We will assess," I ask them to investigate the distance they are placing themselves from "doing" or "changing" by "studying" and "assessing."

So when we talk about our obstacles and the most common verb is "to overcome," it tell us something. It tells us we aren't friends with our obstacles but are battling them, that we aren't learning from them but beating them, that we aren't embracing them but killing them.

What if we befriended them, instead?

Morning: What obstacles are keeping you from your dream right now? List them.

Evening: Once you have your list of obstacles, note beside them the action you can take to befriend them.

July 24

"The bamboo that bends is stronger than the oak that resists."

—JAPANESE PROVERB

Just as buildings sway in earthquakes and bamboo gives in to strong winds to avoid snapping in two, we intellectually know we need to bend. But in moments of stress, we grow rigid. Our bodies betray our minds and we freeze up, unbending, brittle, on the verge of snapping.

What will it take for you to acknowledge your own resiliency? We had it as children, tumbling and falling with great ease, breaking bones and bouncing back quickly without a story of woe attached to it.

Relax into the fall. You will bend. You are resilient.

Morning: Today, try to feel resiliency in your body—what does it feel like? Is it a looseness you can embody? Is there a way you can remind yourself to bend?

Evening: Embody this fully—stretch this evening. Incorporate stretching into your daily ritual, in such a way building bendiness and resiliency.

July 25

"What we do see depends mainly on what we look for. . . . In the same field the farmer will notice the crop, the geologists the fossils, botanists the flowers, artists the coloring, sportmen the cover for the game. Though we may all look at the same things, it does not all follow that we should see them."

—JOHN LUBBOCK

When I was chosen to be an exchange student in Sri Lanka, I had never heard of that country (or Ceylon, as it was formerly called). Once I was chosen to go there, I saw it everywhere. You have experienced the same phenomenon, I'm sure.

What happens when we look for possibility? We find it. For kindness? We find that too. And what happens when we look for proof of man's inhumanity to man? We find that.

Your eye and mind and brain are lenses—you get to focus them; make that focus on something you want more of, not on something you want less of in your life.

Morning: What are you looking for today? Naming that intention will determine what you see. Play around with this notion today.

Evening: What did you discover about the intention of seeing?

July 26

Create a Place of BEing.

"It doesn't matter whom you love or where you move from or to, you always take yourself with you. If you don't know who you are, or if you've forgotten or misplaced her, then you'll always feel as if you don't belong. Anywhere."

—SARAH BAN BREATHNACH

I have traveled around the world, to places like and quite unlike my life in the United States. And I have always felt at home. Why? Because I took my full self with me.

What if your place is inseparable from you? What if you are your own place? We carry ourselves around, and in spite of that movement to foreign places, we are always at home in ourselves—or we are not. Wisdom sits in places, the Navajo remind us—what does it mean to fully embody ourselves and in so doing, fully embody the places we inhabit?

Morning: What does it feel like to fully inhabit a place? Have you had that feeling? If so, when? If not, what has kept you from it?

Evening: Creating a place of being requires being in this moment, not waiting for the next move. How easy or hard is that for you?

July 27

"And falling's just another way to fly."

—EMILIE AUTUMN

What does falling teach us?

To slow down.

To get back up.

To look around while we're down there.

To pick something up while we're down.

To hear what secrets the leaves are telling to the wind as they dance, which looks a lot like falling to the untrained eye.

Morning: What does "falling" look like in your life? Is it always equated with failure? Can you equate it with exploration instead? With dancing?

Evening: What if falling were necessary to survival? How might you look at falling then?

July 28

"*There was something unmistakably exultant about the mess that Rosa had made. Her bedroom-studio was at once the canvas, journal, museum, and midden of her life. She did not 'decorate' it; she infused it.*"

—MICHAEL CHABON

I once went into our backyard to find a fully clothed Tess sitting in a large flowerpot covered with mud, water still pouring out of the hose she held above her head, with one of the biggest smiles I've ever seen. "That is one fine mess," I said, making her smile even more.

Emma decided when she was a teenager that she needed a dark burgundy room with a brown ceiling and a silver door. Her grandmother was aghast: "You're *not* going to let her do that, are you? What if you ever try to sell the house?"

"What if the moon explodes?" I thought to myself. I'll bet you can imagine the outcome. She loved that dark, dark room.

Sometimes, there is nothing so important as a good mess.

Morning: Get messy today. Let yourself get dirty. Spill things, walk in mud, have a food fight, make bad art.

Evening: How did that feel?

"Start where you are. Use what you have. Do what you can."

—ARTHUR ASHE

I can think of no better advice. Ashe doesn't say, "Get somewhere else before you start" or "Get more supplies" or "Learn a new skill."

He says start. Here. With what you have already.

Go.

Morning: I've often said that it's the starting that stops you. Don't let it—start. Not after you have a new notebook or the right pen. Not after you take another class. Now.

Evening: What if you said this to yourself every single morning: "I have what I need."

Stretch your imagination.

"*I like nonsense, it wakes up the brain cells. Fantasy is a necessary ingredient in living, it's a way of looking at life through the wrong end of a telescope. Which is what I do, and that enables you to laugh at life's realities.*"

—DR. SEUSS

Imagine your imagination as a canvas.
   And the world as your stretcher boards.
   Start stretching. And start painting.

Morning: What can you see beyond today? How can you stretch beyond what you know today, to what you can only imagine?

Evening: How large is your canvas now?

Storyteller Andy Offutt Irwin has said, "Don't be afraid to be amazing."

Do you feel the power of paying attention to your life? Are rhythms of knowing emerging for you? Is the kind of attentiveness you've been offering your life with each daily rock scary to you? If it is, I'll echo Irwin: Don't be afraid to be amazing.

What is waiting for you, amazing human, is a depth of experience that can sustain you, if you let it.

August

"People of our time are losing the power of celebration. Instead of celebrating, we seek to be amused or entertained. Celebration is an active state, an act of expressing reverence or appreciation. To be entertained is a passive state—it is to receive pleasure afforded by an amusing act or a spectacle. . . . Celebration is a confrontation, giving attention to the transcendent meaning of one's actions."

—ABRAHAM JOSHUA HESCHEL

At the end of Tess's camp one summer, families of the campers gathered for their talent show. Some kids sang, some built things from Legos, some at the last moment couldn't be persuaded to move from their chairs to participate. It didn't matter. In their own way, they each made a strong offer. And so did their counselors. Each counselor had created an award for their camper that mirrored the camper's interests and celebrated what they had done during that week. Those awards meant "I see you. I really see you."

Morning: Do you know someone at work who always lightens the mood? Make them an award for that and give it to them today. Is there someone at your apartment building who keeps it looking beautiful? Give that man or woman an award! Imagine if we all did this every day. A world of people being seen.

Evening: Can you create a weekly practice of this?

August 1

"That word is 'willing.' It's an attitude and spirit of cooperation that should permeate our conversations. It's like a palm tree by the ocean that endures the greatest winds because it knows how to gracefully bend."

—STEPHEN KENDRICK

Willingness is an opening up, too, isn't it? It is arms flung open, even if quietly, softly, gently. Willingness is not loud or needy. Willingness doesn't insist upon itself or yell or need to be acknowledged. Then it's not willingness, but performance. Instead, it gracefully bends toward the sun. Let this sweet spirit of willingness—to hear someone out, to be open to other options, to let someone else choose, to become a beginner again—permeate your conversations today. Bend.

Morning: How can you lean into willingness today, instead of shutting down? It's often more expedient to shut down, we believe. It saves time, we think. But in the long term, it damages relationships. Be willing to listen today.

Evening: If you were creating a sculpture of willingness, what would it look like? Can you feel that in your body tomorrow?

August 2

"If you were born without wings, do nothing to prevent them from growing."

—COCO CHANEL

A famous astronomer once said, "Keep looking up!" to Emma. It's good advice for all of us.

Oprah once granted the "wildest dreams" of women from her audience. Afterward, she noted how small those dreams were—we need to dream bigger for ourselves, she said. I wonder why we settle for less than stardust?

Are we afraid of falling from such a great height? Don't we know that the universe will catch us? Can't we see that the view on the way down will be spectacular?

What rainbow have you clutched? Have you been too earth-bound, too small, too contained in your wildest dreams? Keep looking up, wherever "up" is to you.

Morning: What is your "up"? What star are you reaching for?

Evening: Who needs your encouragement to reach for the stars? How can you give that to them?

August 3

Name Your intention.

"The life of every man is a diary in which he means to write one story, and writes another."

—J. M. BARRIE

Your life is either run by circumstance or intention. You get to choose which one is the North Star. Some choose (either intentionally or by default) to have themselves blown about by the winds of circumstance—letting their desires and plans be obliterated by external events. They become victims to what is outside themselves and start using the language of victims: "I couldn't create the life I wanted because the economy crashed [insert disaster here]." Others choose (intentionally) to acknowledge that circumstances are sometimes beyond their control, and sometimes not healthy or supportive of their dreams—but they dream anyway. And they use the language of intention: "I cannot change this circumstance, but I am 100 percent in control of how I *am* in that circumstance."

Morning: Today, notice if you are acting out of intention or circumstance. How would it feel to be intention-driven?

Evening: Do you know your intention in life? How can you know it, if not by living into it?

August 4

"Silence is the best way to confabulate with the unseen."

—MICHAEL BASSEY JOHNSON

Wikipedia defines "daydreaming" as "a short-term detachment from one's immediate surroundings, during which a person's contact with reality is blurred and partially substituted by a visionary fantasy, especially one of happy, pleasant thoughts, hopes or ambitions, imagined as coming to pass, and experienced while awake."

Daydreaming has gotten a bad rap over the years—by teachers, by Freud, and others. Yet at its base it is simply a freedom to create outside the confines of place and time. This dissociative space allows us the silence to "confabulate with the unseen," to image what might be.

Morning: Do you give yourself time to daydream? If not, why not?

Evening: Sit for ten minutes looking out your window without a goal in mind. Lose yourself in silence.

August 5

"*Nothing in the world is permanent, and we're foolish when we ask anything to last, but surely we're still more foolish not to take delight in it while we have it.*"

—W. SOMERSET MAUGHAM

Once while working in Hastings, Nebraska, my hosts took me to a pizza restaurant for dinner, a place with a racecar theme. When the waitress put my personal pizza in front of me, I looked down and saw it had been served on a tire. Imagine my delight! I was so surprised that I squealed, to the amusement of my hosts who had seen it many times.

It feels great to be delighted—such a rush of happy! When is the last time you let yourself feel delighted? To feel it, we have to be willing to let go of our demure knowing, our worldliness. Can you?

Morning: Prepare to be delighted today—look for opportunities to squeal.

Evening: What did you discover today about being delighted? What keeps you from it?

August 6

Just Be you.

"Letting go of 'stuff' allowed the world to collapse behind me as I moved, so I became nothing more or less than who I simply was: Me."

—DEE WILLIAMS

If you were enough just as you are, nobody would have a "hook" in you to buy from them. We are bombarded with messages of need so often—you *need* this belly crème to eliminate stretch marks, you *need* this special blender, you *need* to . . . the list is endless.

What if the message was, "You are fantastically you. Don't stop being you."

There is a direct correlation between consumerism and having an unhealthy self-image. We are being trained for "need."

Morning: Pay attention to the messages you get today about what you need to be fully, authentically, more beautifully you. Make a list of them.

Evening: Create a spending moratorium for yourself of at least a month. In that time, pay attention to messages of need and note how it feels to say "no."

Create new patterns.

"From where we stand the rain seems random. If we could stand somewhere else, we would see the order in it."

—TONY HILLERMAN

It's not easy to see our patterns, much less create new, healthier ones.

To do that, we have to stand somewhere else, as Hillerman suggests.

Morning: What is an unhealthy pattern you have that you'd like to change?

Evening: Where will you need to stand to see that pattern more clearly in order to change it?

August 8

"What sunshine is to flowers, smiles are to humanity. These are but trifles, to be sure, but scattered along life's pathway, the good they do is inconceivable."

–JOSEPH ADDISON

This one is simple. Smile more.
    Offer smiles to people you know and don't know.
    See what happens.
    Then smile some more.

Morning: Smile at everyone you meet today.

Evening: What did you discover about smiling?

August 9

"A burden shared is a burden halved."

—T. A. WEBB

We all carry burdens with us: How to care for our children or aging parents. The shame of a past mistake we try to keep hidden. Financial stress.

Shame and vulnerability keep us silent about these weights we carry around with us, and they will keep us from living fully. Until recently, I had never shared any of our struggles to help Tess with her Asperger's syndrome. When I did, a thunderous show of support emerged—people sharing their own experiences, and just showing up for us.

Let people help.

Morning: Imagine you are Sisyphus, rolling that big stone up the hill over and over again. Let someone help you shoulder the stone.

Evening: How does it feel to share the burden? Is it difficult to ask for help? Is there a sense of relief after you do so?

August 10

check in
with those
you love.

"Our lives disconnect and reconnect, we move on, and later we may again touch one another, again bounce away. This is the felt shape of a human life, neither simply linear nor wholly disjunctive nor endlessly bifurcating, but rather this bouncey-castle sequence of bumpings-into and tumblings-apart."

—SALMAN RUSHDIE

We bump up against many people in this carnival we call life. Sometimes we find people whom we learn to love, and sometimes we lose them in the bouncy castle.

Today, check in with a few of them. Reconnect if only for a moment.

Morning: With whom would you like to check in? Do it today.

Evening: How did it feel to check in?

August 11

"You can dance in the storm. Don't wait for the rain to be over before because it might take too long. You can do it now. Wherever you are, right now, you can start, right now; this very moment."

—ISRAELMORE AYIVOR

Dance in the storm.
 Start now.
 Remember: Inaction *is* a decision.

Morning: What do you want to do? How can you start it now?

Evening: Rein in your impulse control this week and let loose. Do it now, without apologies or disclaimers that you're not ready.

August 12

Ignore what People say.

"... here's what I've learned—people will hurt you, but you don't have to respond—not every mean comment or cruel act deserves to be noticed ..."

–JOHN GEDDES

I once was accused of defaming someone in an article I wrote. They sent a five-page letter outlining why they were going to sue me. It was a case totally without merit, but I felt I needed to respond, so I wrote a five-page letter in response, asking a lawyer friend to review it before I sent it. My friend, Larry, read it and called me the next day. "This is amazing," he said. "Great job! I especially like the part where you say 'Dear Jerry' and the part where you say 'Sincerely, Patti,' and I would take out everything in the middle."

"But . . . but . . . I have to respond!"

"No," Larry said. "You don't."

The most powerful person in a tug-of-war is the person who doesn't pick up his or her end of the rope.

Morning: Can you let go of your end of the rope today?

Evening: How does it feel to let go of that rope?

August 13

"Don't go where the path may lead, go instead where there is no path . . . and leave a trail."

—RALPH WALDO EMERSON

In high school, I went on a weeklong hike from Table Rock to Mt. Mitchell in North Carolina. Because the students were the orienteers, we spent a fair amount of time lost. "Let's leave crumbs along the way so we can find our way back," someone suggested, the urge being toward "found-ness."

"Our job on the trail," one of the counselors reminded us, "is to leave no trace."

And for the longest time, these two impulses have seemed at odds for me: Leave a trail or leave no trace. But I think this is a both/and equation: Leave a trail that leaves no trace.

Morning: Imagine your impact as the wake from a speedboat—what kind of wake are you making?

Evening: Are you leaving a trail so others can follow you, or so you can get out?

August 14

I grew up as a perfectionist. The messages I heard as a child included: "If you want something done right, do it yourself." And "Do the job right the first time." Perfectionism breeds all-or-nothing thinking, and an almost certain paralysis. What if we strove for excellence instead, creating in ourselves a healthy anxiety with a destination rather than an overwhelming need for perfection?

Morning: What is "good enough"?

Evening: How does perfectionism have an impact on your life?

August 15

"Be like water making its way through cracks. Do not be assertive, but adjust to the object, and you shall find a way round or through it. If nothing within you stays rigid, outward things will disclose themselves. Empty your mind, be formless. Shapeless, like water. If you put water into a cup, it becomes the cup. You put water into a bottle and it becomes the bottle. You put it in a teapot, it becomes the teapot. Now, water can flow or it can crash. Be water, my friend."

—BRUCE LEE

Resiliency is a flow, a springing back. In some contexts the word is used to mean the strength to resist the impact of an adverse event, but more true to its Latin roots, "resiliency" is the "capacity to rebound" or the "act of rebounding" from adversity. There is a big difference between "resistance" and "resilience." They are, in effect, two different actions, one pushing against (static) and one bouncing back from (dynamic).

Resisting is rigid. In resisting adversity, your dreams shatter rather than bounce back. They crash. Resiliency is fluid. In rebounding from adversity, your dreams flow.

Morning: Be water, my friend.

Evening: Notice how many times your first impulse is to resist tomorrow—shift the focus to rebound, instead.

August 16

"We do not grow absolutely, chronologically. We grow sometimes in one dimension, and not in another; unevenly. We grow partially. We are relative. We are mature in one realm, childish in another. The past, present, and future mingle and pull us backward, forward, or fix us in the present. We are made up of layers, cells, constellations."

—ANAÏS NIN

It's interesting to think about our lives as layers, strata of emotion and body and events, like the cut-open side of a mountain where we can see the different colors of earth, each building upon the one below, the one inside. While we might prefer to hate or get rid of or deny some layers, they are vital to the whole, keeping the cake from collapsing, the mountain from crumbling.

Morning: Love all those layers, the mature, the childish, the past, the present, eliminating none of them, but acknowledging their important presence in our lives.

Evening: If you drew the strata of your life, what would they look like? Find out.

August 17

And the depth of it. What does it mean to live deeper? Some
might say it means to dig harder. I think it means to dig less
and be more present where you are. Some might say it means to
seek more answers. I think it means to ask more questions and
have that be enough. Some might say it means to eschew things
on the surface of life. I think it means to find meaning in those
things.

Morning: How will you live deeper and wider?

Evening: What does it take to dive in?

August 18

create spaciousness.

"These trees are magnificent, but even more magnificent is the sublime and moving space between them, as though with their growth it too increased."

—RAINER MARIA RILKE

Last year we moved, after eleven years in our home. We didn't box everything up and move it—we got rid of half of what we owned, or more. We simplified to create spaciousness in our lives, trading belongings for experiences, opening the flow in our lives again, breaking the dam of ownership that had clogged our house.

We all need to breathe, to allow for the space between those trees, as Rilke said.

Clear something out. Give something you have loved to someone who needs in their life now what it represented to you then. Clear the space in order to grow, like those trees of which Rilke speaks.

Morning: Today, let go of thirty-seven things: objects, stories, limiting beliefs, grudges, socks with no mates. Make a list and count them up, to thirty-seven. Breathe in the new space you have created.

Evening: What can you let go of tomorrow?

August 19

*"People are forever watching things. They should be
seeing. I see the things I look at. I am a see-er."*

—PATRICK ROTHFUSS

You know those iconic photographs so many of us recognize?
Those scenes from shared human history that are seared into
our collective memories? The flag-raising at Iwo Jima, the
young man in front of the tank at Tiananmen Square, the exe-
cution of Nguyễn Văn Lém by Nguyễn Ngọc Loan during the
Vietnam War, and so many more.

My husband, John, is always more interested in turning
around to look at the watchers, the scene behind the camera. I
love that about him. And I have finally learned that from him.
On a business trip a few years ago, I stood on the balcony of
my hotel room and took photos of a spectacular Florida sunset.
Only when I turned to go back into the room did I realize that
the more beautiful vision was behind me, the big puffy clouds
onto which the sunset was reflected as onto a screen. There is
something more than what we see.

Morning: Turn around, look.

Evening: Now try to go deeper: Turn around, see.

August 20

"If you need encouragement, praise, pats on the back from everybody, then you make everybody your judge."

—FRITZ PERLS

Barbara Kingsolver spoke in Asheville, North Carolina, where I lived at the time, and told the audience that she doesn't read any reviews of her work. "When I was a young writer," she explained, "I read every review and realized I was ignoring the good ones and memorizing the bad ones."

Are you creating things to make critics happy? Is that really the highest and best use of your life force, your creative spark, your soul, that big brain your body carries around? I think not.

Make strong offers. Ignore the critics—it drives them crazy.

Morning: Put your work into the world and let it stand on its own. Your work is done—move on.

Evening: There is a difference between learning from criticism and being paralyzed by it—which are you?

August 21

"Dance is the hidden language of the soul."

—MARTHA GRAHAM

Feel self-conscious about dancing? Me, too. It didn't used to be that way. Every Friday night in high school, I was on the dance floor with my friend Steve, doing elaborate disco moves (stop laughing). I haven't danced like that—with abandon and joy and passion—in years. Decades. So I'm heeding this rock.

Self-conscious? Do it anyway. In private, if need be. Without mirrors, if you must. Just move your body. Put on music you love and move. Move. No other experience needed. No disco balls, no dance floor, just you in your bathroom or bedroom swaying (or moving more dramatically if you're up to it). Music is elemental: Earth, Water, Air, Fire—and Music. It grounds us to the earth and lifts us up to the sky. It heats us and satisfies our thirst, music does. The corollary to music is movement. It, too, grounds us, lifts us, heats us, and satisfies us.

Move today. With music. Call it dance, or not. Just move.

Morning: Put on the radio. Move for five minutes as you get ready for the day. You've done this activity twice before in *Your Daily Rock*—it's that important.

Evening: How can you incorporating dancing into your life?

August 22

"The most powerful weapon on earth is the human soul on fire."

—FERDINAND FOCH

My friend Lisa Evans taught me this. It changes things: When you meet someone, don't ask them, "What do you do?" Instead, ask them, "What do you *love* to do?" The difference is palpable, heart-filled; it is a question that opens space rather than closing it down. It allows people to tell you about their passions instead of being pinned like a butterfly to a board by a job title that might not reflect that deeper them, the part that sustains them and makes them fully human.

Morning: Today, ask the people you see, "What do you love to do?"

Evening: In what ways did this question change the quality of your engagement?

August 23

*"It's humbling to start fresh. It takes a lot of courage.
But it can be reinvigorating. You just have to put
your ego on a shelf and tell it to be quiet."*

—JENNIFER RITCHIE PAYETTE

Every day is day one.

Every single one. So you screwed up your wellness plan today
with a frosted cherry Pop-Tart? Sit with the "why" of that and
then recognize that tomorrow is day one. Every day's sunrise
brings with it a bright fresh canvas, an open space for renewal,
for newness, for doing what you intended to do, for being in
this very moment a bundle of pure possibility.

Breathe in possibility today. And tomorrow.

Morning: What fresh start do you want or need today? In what
ways can you put your ego on a shelf in order to make that fresh
start?

Evening: How does ego get in the way of your do-overs?

August 24

"Be kind whenever possible. It is always possible."

—DALAI LAMA

Be kind. Be kind. Be kind.

This one is simple: Be kind. Especially when kindness is the harder choice.

Morning: Consciously choose kindness today.

Evening: How does it feel to make that choice?

August 25

"We build too many walls and not enough bridges."

—ISAAC NEWTON

What is a bridge? What does a bridge do? I had a powerful conversation about those two questions in a class I was teaching one summer. We drew bridges to remind ourselves of their structure. We talked about what we know about bridges: They connect things, they span distances, they make reaching other places possible, they are able to bear great weight, they have to expand and contract and respond to the wind, they are stable because they are well grounded, and—ultimately—they are well grounded in a shared earth, however separated those ends are by a great distance. So, too, with the bridges between humans.

Morning: How can you build a bridge instead of a wall today?

Evening: What walls needed to come down to make that bridge possible?

August 26

"Darkness cannot drive out darkness: only light can do that.
Hate cannot drive out hate: only love can do that."

—MARTIN LUTHER KING JR.

We have a choice to open up, or shut down; to love or to hate. Every day we have that choice: to protect our hearts or to fling them open so they can fulfill their highest purpose: to love. I hope we can choose love. Because at the end of it, love is what's left.

When in doubt, love.

Morning: As you go through your day today, you will have choices—to love or not to love. Use this question to help determine the direction your day (and life) will take: What would love do?

Evening: How does a closed heart feel? An open one?

August 27

"Making a dream into reality begins with what you have, not with what you are waiting on."

—T. F. HODGE

Here's the deal. We're always in abundance. There is no lack—because either we are adding up our blessings or our troubles. Either way, we have an abundance, of one or the other. You get to choose which one you want to count, and that becomes the true measure of your life.

Morning: What are you counting?

Evening: Can you feel the abundance in your life right now? Because if you can't, no future abundance will satisfy you either.

August 28

"Stories make us more alive, more human, more courageous, more loving."

—MADELEINE L'ENGLE

I'm slightly addicted to watching first auditions for *The X Factor* on YouTube. What I love is knowing even just a small part of the backstory for the song they have chosen . . . because that story changes the experience of listening to them sing.

It is clear to me that the shortest distance between two people is a story. If I know your story, I can connect with you at a deeper level, from a place of deeper understanding, and perhaps even from a place of knowing, of recognition. When I know your story, you become a "who" to me, and not just a "what." Categories break down, dissolve.

They make us who we are. And they connect us in ways we can hardly imagine. Tell them your story. And listen to theirs.

Morning: Whose stories do you need to hear? To whom do you need to tell your story? Perhaps the first step is to tell yourself your own story.

Evening: Seek out stories like you might seek out gold. That's what they are. We are made of stories.

August 29

Nurture your creative spirit.

"When we treat children's play as seriously as it deserves, we are helping them feel the joy that's to be found in the creative spirit. It's the things we play with and the people who help us play that make a great difference in our lives."

—FRED ROGERS

When we lose touch with our creative spirit, it's because we've lost the capacity to play, to stand barefoot in grass, to blow bubbles, to explore what makes us laugh, and laugh, and laugh. Mr. Rogers knew what it was to tap into our creative spirit. When's the last time you played?

Morning: What keeps you from playing? Notice that today.

Evening: What can you do to free yourself from those things that deflect you from play in your life?

August 30

"Get close to grass and you'll see a star."

—DEJAN STOJANOVIĆ

Every day, unless there is snow on the ground (I'm Southern; we don't do snow), I make it a point to stand on the grass, barefoot, even if just for a minute. Typically, I stand there five minutes unless it is very cold.

There is something special about feeling grass, matching foot to earth—a groundedness and a calm.

We have separated ourselves from the earth in so many ways; it is time to reconnect.

Morning: Stand outside on the grass for five minutes today; lie down in it if you can.

Evening: How did it feel to be on the earth? Can you make this a daily practice? If not, keep it in mind as a way to calm yourself in times of stress.

August 31

Another month that feels like a fresh start. The beginning of a new season. Regroup, shed what is not serving you. Declutter your brain. Start writing with a new pen in a new notebook. Let things fall away that don't feel sustainable and sustaining.

Recommit to your daily practice. Even if you are in resistance to it, don't stop there—play with your resistance and learn from it rather than letting it stop you. Walk hand in hand with it rather than running from it.

Restart.

September

"A finite game is played for the purpose of winning, an infinite game for the purpose of continuing the play."

—JAMES P. CARSE

A book I keep going back to is James Carse's *Finite and Infinite Games*. Why? Because he describes two ways of being in the world that we all fall into—we are either playing life to win or playing life to learn.

Football is a finite game—the whole point is to have a winner and a loser. Hackeysack is an infinite game—the whole point is to keep the game going.

At every moment, we are operating from a place of win/lose in which "failure" = "lose" or from a place of learning in which "failure" = "learn." It is a choice that greatly affects the quality of our lives, the ways we take risks, or don't, and the ways we allow ourselves to leap, or don't.

Morning: As you go through the moments of your day today, ask yourself this question: Am I playing to win or playing to learn? Shift toward learning.

Evening: How might playing to learn change your life?

September 1

Once, Tess told me she was talking to her heart. I loved that image, and the depth of what that meant to her as she described it to me. "Why, honey? What do you say to your heart?" I asked. "I tell it everything is okay," she said, and skipped away.

Maybe this is a practice I need to start—a conversation with my heart every morning. And a pause to listen to its reply.

Morning: Today, have that conversation with your heart—aloud or on paper. Spell it out. What are you saying to your heart? And what is your heart responding?

Evening: Sit quietly for a few moments and appreciate the rhythm of your heart in your chest, and the ways in which that rhythm means life itself. Take care of this engine—converse with it daily.

September 2

"Those who do not weep, do not see."

—VICTOR HUGO

Once when my father was in the hospital, he had a lot of gas as the result of a medical procedure, and was ever the gentleman, apologizing to the nurses when a fart would escape even after he had tried holding it in. "Honey," one nurse said after he apologized, "you let it out. There is a lot more room out here than there is in there and you'll hurt yourself if you keep it in."

So, too, with tears.

What are we missing if we do not weep? And what do we do instead of weep? Singer Jahméne Douglas has a nervous giggle that comes out at the end of almost everything he says. Why? Because his father used to beat him and he wasn't allowed to cry, so he developed the giggle as a coping mechanism.

Morning: There is a lot more room outside. Let those tears out.

Evening: We get so many messages about crying—that it isn't professional, that boys don't cry, that big girls don't cry. What are the messages you've received in your life about crying? What is your safety net, like Jahméne's giggle?

September 3

"Stay open, forever, so open it hurts, and then open up some more, until the day you die, world without end, amen."

—GEORGE SAUNDERS

Shutting down is closing off, stopping, shrinking, reducing, protecting. It is easy to do, but the costs can be high. Choose the braver path, the path that opens to possibility, and yes, to hurt.

Reductive or generative.

Safe or bold.

Finite or infinite.

Yes, but, or *Yes, and.*

You choose.

Morning: How can you stay open today?

Evening: How does it feel to be open? To be shut down? Which one gives you hope, and which sadness? Which one challenges you, and which smothers you?

September 4

"Be selective in your battles; sometimes peace is better than being right."

—RITU GHATOUREY

The things you are arguing about, that you are asserting as true and right? Those things can be both true *and* false, depending on where you stand.

Imagine this: What is most true in all the arguments we have about right and wrong is that our attachment to rightness is what is hurting us, rather than the issue itself. Our attachment to being right is as much an attachment as owning something . . . we hold on to it ferociously and to be happy we need to give up that need to be right.

It is harder to do than it seems. Why? Because we are right. And yes, even then, especially then, we need to choose peace rather than being right. Choose happy rather than right.

Morning: This is a process of letting go. What "rightness" can you let go of today?

Evening: Do you still feel the need to say, "Yes, but I'm right?" Work at it again tomorrow. Let go.

September 5

"We all do things we desperately wish we could undo. Those regrets just become part of who we are, along with everything else. To spend time trying to change that, well, it's like chasing clouds."

—LIBBA BRAY

I have long believed that regret is the most powerful human emotion. I have waged war with regret, but now I realize my regrets are as much a part of me as my blood vessels or lungs—they make me who I am, and they sustain life, in some way.

Yes, I regret things I've done or not done. We all do. Some of those regrets make our faces flush with hotness when we think of them. Some make us weep. These are as natural as that blood beating through our blood vessels or the expansion of our lungs. Each beat of our lives is vital and life-giving.

Morning: Which regrets make your face hot and your chest hollow? See them as the clouds above you today. Those clouds move on. Let's.

Evening: Make a list of your life's regrets. Fully own each one, for once. And tomorrow imagine they are always with you as clouds—beautiful, sometimes dark, shielding you from the sun at times. Just as beautiful as a cloud.

September 6

your body
is your
autobiography

We act sometimes as if our bodies are simply vehicles to carry our big heads around, but they are so, so much more.

If you drew a map of your body, what would it tell you?

Morning: Draw an outline of your body. Mark where you have pain, where you feel lust, where secrets are held, where you have been cut open, where the stories are that you've never told anyone. Mark where you have been violated or treasured. You are walking around with all this, all day, every day. Let that be a beautiful map in which scars are seams between pieces, codas between chapters in your autobiography.

Evening: Sit with your map. What would you add?

September 7

sit in the garden.

"You are sitting on the earth and you realize that this earth deserves you and you deserve this earth. You are there—fully, personally, genuinely."

—CHÖGYAM TRUNGPA

My friend Kichom Hayashi used to tell me that he needed to go be in nature more, that he found answers there.

When is the last time you sat in the garden?

Morning: Sit on the earth today. Sink into it.

Evening: Every day this week, go barefoot on the earth, even if just to stand on a small patch of grass outside your home or work. Feel yourself on the earth.

September 8

"You are the Hero of your own Story."

—JOSEPH CAMPBELL

Being a hero seems daunting. Perhaps Joseph Campbell might have suggested that we are an interesting main character with a few key flaws, or even a bit actor who stumbled onto the set and had good hair so they made him the star.

But a hero? Whoa. That's a lot of responsibility.

Until we realize what a hero is: Romain Rolland has said, "A hero is a man who does what he can."

That's all. Do what you can. Nobody can ask more of you than that.

Morning: What kind of hero will you be today?

Evening: Did you do what you could today?

September 9

*"'I just wanted to thank you,' he says, his voice low. 'A group of scientists
told you that my genes were damaged, that there was something wrong with
me—they showed you the test results that proved it. And even I started to
believe it.' He touches my face, his thumb skimming my cheekbone, and
his eyes are on mine, intense and insistent. 'You never believed it,' he says.
'Not for a second. You always insisted I was . . . I don't know, whole.'"*

—VERONICA ROTH

You have the capacity to tell a story of wholeness about someone
else—or a story of brokenness.

And in exactly the same way, you have the capacity to tell a
story of wholeness about yourself—or a story of brokenness.

All of us have these two choices every day. Which one will
you invest in? Wholeness or brokenness?

Morning: Notice the stories you tell today about yourself and
others—which are they?

Evening: When you think of the stories of brokenness that you
tell, how can you reframe those as stories of wholeness?

September 10

"All relaxation does is allow the truth to be felt. The mind is cleared, like a dirty window wiped clean, and the magnitude of what we might ordinarily take for granted inspires tears."

—JAY MICHAELSON

Whew. I see the truth in this quote.

Is this why we have such a hard time relaxing? We go on vacation tethered to our phones and laptops, seeking Wi-Fi like addicts. We only schedule one business call during our time away, congratulating ourselves on our restraint.

Stop.

Let your mind be cleared so you can see what is really important. Allow the truth of your life to be deeply felt. Don't run away from it, like you are running to get the only free electrical outlet in the airport lounge.

Stop.

Morning: When is the last time you let yourself truly relax?

Evening: What truth are you afraid of finding?

September 11

*"It is the greatest of all mistakes to do nothing because
you can only do little—do what you can."*

—SYDNEY SMITH

Imagine someone who is embarking on a long journey; storms
have cluttered their way with debris. We can't take the journey
for them, or even with them, sometimes. Theirs is a solitary
journey in this moment. We feel helpless. What can we do to
help? Nothing, it seems. The need seems too big and any action
we can take seems too insignificant.

Sometimes the most we can do is clear the way for others to
walk their own path, take their own journey. Sweep the portion
of their path we can—clear the debris as best we can.

I love this simple, beautiful image of sweeping a path for
someone.

Morning: How can you sweep a beautiful path for others today?

Evening: Imagine your life as a path. What can you allow others
to sweep from that path to clear your way?

September 12

"Celebrate what you want to see more of."

—TOM PETERS

It is easy to grow up well honed in the art of criticizing. We get rewarded for "critical thinking," particularly in our workplaces, far more than we are rewarded for celebrating. Celebration can even be seen as naive or Pollyanna-ish. But in our rush to prove we can think critically, we forget that we see what we expect to see. If we look for what is wrong, we will find it. If we look for things to celebrate, we will find them instead.

Morning: What do you want to see more of? Make a list.

Evening: Review your list and celebrate those things when they appear in your life. They will begin to multiply.

September 13

"Slow down and enjoy life. It's not only the scenery you miss by going too fast—you also miss the sense of where you are going and why."

—EDDIE CANTOR

We are moving too fast to really see. We don't often sit still long enough to watch the world around us—we are too driven to jump into that stream. Sit on the bank.

See the bees fly by you, the flowers unfold. See your children wiggle their loose teeth and be nervous and excited about that moment when they will fall out.

Walk in the rain and watch the reflection of clouds in puddles. Really see. Not dizzy flashes of life moving by as if you're on an interstate, but something altogether different.

Morning: Take the slow road today. Reach out to the world with your arms open.

Evening: What did you really see today?

September 14

"You can find something truly important in an ordinary minute."

—MITCH ALBOM

On special occasions, we pull out our best china and those really beautiful and impossibly thin-sided glasses that Grandma got when she was married long, long ago. And while we save our best china for special occasions, being alive is really the special occasion.

Morning: Pull out the fancy china for breakfast today.

Evening: And for dinner, too.

September 15

"There are four questions of value in life. . . . What is sacred?
Of what is the spirit made? What is worth living for, and what is
worth dying for? The answer to each is the same. Only love."

—JOHNNY DEPP

Oh, it is a fine day when Johnny Depp is quoted in a book of mine.

What is your deepest experience of love?

What is sacred in your life?

What do you live for? And what would you die for?

Is it possible to look beyond the surface of each of your answers to find that, in fact, love is at the root of them?

Morning: What questions can love not answer?

Evening: What is the power of love in your life? What would you like it to be?

September 16

"There's a lot of fear connected with the inner journey because it penetrates our illusions. Taking the inner journey will lead you into some very shadowy places. You're going to learn things about yourself that you'll wish you didn't know. There are monsters in there—monsters you can't control— but trying to keep them hidden will only give them greater power."

—PARKER PALMER

If you have a big fear about a monster, one of the best things you can do is write a story for children about how to get over that fear. That forces us to explain it in simple, engaging, story terms, and provide guidance—which can be just as useful for us, the writer, as for our audience.

Go on that inner journey, look in the dark corners, and in so doing, lessen the power of the monsters. Write about those monsters—how would you tell a child to befriend them?

Morning: What do you fear knowing about yourself? How does that fear show up in your life or body?

Evening: What light can you take with you on your inner journey?

September 17

"When we give cheerfully and accept gratefully, everyone is blessed."

—MAYA ANGELOU

A few years ago, a relative of mine needed help with what appeared to be an addiction to prescription drugs. I asked friends their opinion on the differences between "interference" and "intervention" and one man wrote back with a suggestion of knowing in my heart what "right helpfulness" would do.

Right helpfulness. It is a phrase that made me look beyond my action to the needs of the other person. It made me seek answers to deeper questions. What is my reason for wanting to do something about this? Does that serve them, or just me? Do I just want to be right about this?

The golden rule is beautiful, and sometimes falls short of recognizing the complexities of our lives—what *I* need is not what *you* need. So perhaps lending a hand comes with this question: "What would be most helpful to you at this moment?" without assuming that our own expertise or desires or preferences are what is needed.

Morning: Do we only feel compelled to give when we feel we are lifting someone else up? Or is there a more complex, equal human dynamic that can be part of this equation of helpfulness?

Evening: Are you a grateful giver and receiver?

September 18

"What happens when people open their hearts?" . . .
"They get better."

—HARUKI MURAKAMI

There is nothing wrong with being fragile. We all are, balanced on a tiny point between life and death, between pain and joy, between up and down, on a tiny dot in a big, big universe. All of us. Some people respond to that fragility by being tough, demanding, mean to waitresses, harsh—all in the spirit of showing how strong they are.

But that's not strong; that's wearing a mask to hide our fear. There is no shame in being fragile. It is our shared human condition. Let's let it show, knowing we can be both fragile and resilient—in community.

Morning: What does your "tough" mask look like? What is it hiding?

Evening: What messages have you gotten in your life about being fragile? Which of these messages close your heart to yourself, to others, and to life itself?

September 19

"No one saves us but ourselves. No one can and no one may. We ourselves must walk the path."

—GAUTAMA BUDDHA

I learned this the hard way this year: You have your own flotation device. Don't wait for someone else to save you.

It is so easy to feel like we're not enough, that we need someone to swoop in and save us, make things easier for us, tell us what to do with our business or with our life—and there's no doubt that input can be really valuable, particularly if you seek input from a diverse group. But the only *saving* that can go on is inside you. Having someone else save you is not a business plan or a life plan.

Saving yourself is an inside job, plain and simple. You have what you need to do it.

Morning: What does your flotation device look like? Draw it, or describe it in words—give it shape so you'll know it when you need it.

Evening: When you go on a cruise, there is a mandatory lifeboat drill so you'll know what to do in an emergency—where to find the boat and how to get to it. You've created your flotation device—how will you access it quickly when you need it? Practice doing so.

September 20

"Sometimes it's a form of love just to talk to somebody that you have nothing in common with and still be fascinated by their presence."

—DAVID BYRNE

When I get irritated or "hooked" by someone else's drama (or my own), this is the question I ask myself: What would love do?

I think it would give up being right in the service of being kind. It would step away from righteous and choose satisfied, and even sated. It might even reach out to people who have been unkind. Yes, it would. I think it would likely give away more than it takes. It seems possible that love would trump convenience. It would go out of its way. Love would tell the truth in a way that could be heard and in a way that acknowledges that my truth is not necessarily yours. Love would buoy, not bury. It would open, not close. It would reach toward, not away from. It would move into, not push against. It would create, not collapse. It would never ridicule. Not a neighbor, a stranger, a friend, or the people of Walmart. I'm pretty sure love would hurt sometimes. And heal other times. I think love would make it okay to be less than perfect. Love would open space for other people. Oh, yes, it surely would.

Morning: Today, in moments of stress and shared humanity and irritation, ask, "What would love do?"

Evening: How did that change things?

September 21

"Just breathe. Ten tiny breaths. . . . Seize them. Feel them. Love them."

—K. A. TUCKER

That's all, honey. Because some days, that's all we can do.
  Breathe in: *Hello, moment.* Breathe out: *I am here.*
  Just breathe.

Morning: Set an alarm for every sixty minutes today. When it goes off, spend one minute just breathing and focusing on your breath, saying, "Hello, moment" and "I am here" with each inhalation and exhalation.

Evening: Can breathing be more simple, and more important? It deserves our attention.

September 22

*"I wish I could show you, When you are lonely or in
darkness, The astonishing light of your own being."*

—HAFIZ

We are told so often that we need to be more _____ and more
_____ and more _____. We are bombarded by messages
that tell us we need _____ and _____ and _____.
We tell ourselves if we could only _____ and _____ and
_____, our lives would be better, fuller, more fulfilling,
more _____, more _____, or more _____. Stop.
You, just as you are, in all your beautiful imperfect perfection, are enough. You are enough. Just as you are. Not after you
achieve _____, or lose _____ pounds, or get _____.
Right now.

Morning: Say it out loud: I am enough. Repeat often.

Evening: Tonight, say: I was enough today. And I will be enough
tomorrow.

September 23

"Life is celebration, for those who knows how to celebrate every moment."

—BHARAT ZANVAR

"Have a cupcake" is code for "Let's celebrate!" Because cupcakes are cute and tasty and festive. Perhaps you have your own interpretation of "Let's celebrate!" Maybe your cupcake is "Get a pedicure!" or "Take a personal day to relax!" or "Read a good book!" or "Sit outside and soak in the sunlight."

How do you celebrate? What do you celebrate? Stick a candle in this day and celebrate it—just because life is a celebration.

Morning: Do you wait for special occasions before you celebrate? What if every day deserved a celebration of some kind? What celebration can you have today?

Evening: Every evening, I close the day with a short ritual to celebrate it. The "what" of my ritual isn't important or meaningful to you, but the "why" is. Can you create your own ritual to end and thank each day?

September 24

"Be gentle with yourself. You are a child of the universe no less than the trees and the stars; you have a right to be here."

—MAX EHRMANN

What does gentle look like? It looks like pausing as you look in the mirror to honor what you see, fully aware of the living that has gone on behind those eyeballs, in those hips, and on that skin. It looks like pausing before saying "yes" to another commitment that will exhaust you, and then saying "yes" to yourself instead. It looks like pausing as you cook dinner to feel the satisfying weight of the spoon in your hand. It looks like pausing to read a good book in a big chair. It looks like opening space for yourself to grieve, to love, to long for, to remember, to laugh. It looks like responding to yourself with the kind of patience and unconditional love you extend to friends. It looks like all that, and more.

Morning: How can you be gentle with yourself today?

Evening: And tomorrow?

September 25

"Slow down and enjoy life. It's not only the scenery you miss by going too fast—you also miss the sense of where you are going and why."

—EDDIE CANTOR

One word for you today: Savor.

Savor your food today. Savor the moments outside. Savor each breath you take.

Notice.

Savor.

Morning: When you eat today, have that be the only thing you do—don't watch TV or listen to the radio or answer e-mails while eating. Only eat. Feel the food in your mouth and pay attention to the flavors as if you were going to write a review of the meal for the *New York Times*. Focus on each moment, each bite, each taste.

Evening: Translate that food experience into your life experience: What does it feel like to savor life?

September 26

"Look at everything always as though you were seeing it either for the first or last time: Thus is your time on earth filled with glory."

—BETTY SMITH

Stop trying to be so "sophisticated." And "worldly." And slightly bored with it all.

Don't hide your astonishment. Don't dampen your wonder. Let it loose! Life is amazing! The color of that flower? WOWEE! The sweetness of that red pepper. AWESOME! Don't let your need to be "cool" or "sophisticated" or "in control" take away your capacity to be absolutely wowed by life. So much deserves a YEE-HAW on a daily basis. Run wild with wonder today.

Say wow when you see a bus! A tunnel! A baby! A library book! A stoplight! WOW!

Morning: Look for simple things to be astonished by today. Then express that wonder!

Evening: What impact did wonder have on your day? On your energy level?

September 27

"We've spent so much time judging what other people created that we've created very, very little of our own."

—CHUCK PALAHNIUK

Many of us fear being judged by others so much that we let that fear stop us. We live smaller as a result. Why is this? I think it's directly related to the fact that we judge others. And if we can give up judging others, we can give up our own fear of being judged and live larger.

I think we have a choice every day: We can either judge or learn, but we can't do both at the same time. So if we spend our time judging ourselves or others, we have kicked ourselves out of the capacity to learn something, to take risks, to create.

Most importantly, we are judging our insides by other people's outsides—we don't know the internal struggles they feel by looking at them, nor can they know ours.

Morning: Today when you find yourself making a judgment of any kind—about someone's outfit or choice of meal or idea or accent or choices—pause and release that judgment, and in so doing, free yourself.

Evening: Choose learning over judging.

September 28

(Where "write" is a placeholder for your own passion, your own voice, your own special work in the world.)

"We first make our habits, then our habits make us."

—JOHN DRYDEN

I teach amazing writers. And in our explorations of what it means to write and how to build a sustainable writing practice, it all comes down to sitting back down and staying in the room when the laundry gets real, real fascinating.

Writers write. Painters paint. They create their own practice. And what has taken the place of our work has become our work.

Many writers are busy cleaning their houses and surfing the net instead of writing. There's no judgment implied in that—it is just free data about our priorities and our avoidances. What keeps you from your passion, your work in the world? Whatever it is, *that* has become your work. Is that satisfying to you? Is that your legacy? If not, sit the hell down and write.

Morning: Today, notice when you are distracted by the laundry, by starting a new to-do list. Then stay in the room, sit back down, strengthen your practice.

Evening: Did you notice any patterns about your distractions that can help you "sit down and write"?

September 29

"Freedom lies in being bold."

—ROBERT FROST

I spoke at a retreat recently and the theme of boldness came up.

"I brought bubbles to blow," one woman said. "That's bold for me. That's being on the edge."

What she taught me is that there is no template for bold. Sure, others might believe they are modeling what "bold" is, and they may try to sell us on being their kind of bold, but "bold" is individual. What looks like "bold" for me isn't "bold" for you. And that's fantastic. Bold can be loud, and it can be quiet. Bold can be colorful, and it can be satisfyingly neutral. Bold can be electric, and it can be soft. Bold can be hot, and it can be cool. Bold can be sure, and it can be questioning. Bold can be bubbles to blow.

Be bold in the way that feels like you.

Morning: What does bold look and feel like today for you?

Evening: Tomorrow, work on acknowledging that another person's "bold" might look completely different from your own.

September 30

What if this month was the most important month in your life?

Pay attention as if it is.

See what happens.

October

"The small things of life were often so much bigger than the great things . . . the trivial pleasures like cooking, one's home, little poems especially sad ones, solitary walks, funny things seen and overheard."

—BARBARA PYM

We plan big events, and wait for big moments in our lives. We mark our calendars and polish the silverware and set the table with our grandmother's china. We count down the days. We envision perfection for that moment. And in so doing, we sometimes miss the light on the trees in this perfectly ordinary day.

Morning: Watch the light on the trees today.

Evening: Watch the light on the trees tomorrow.

October 1

"*That is part of the beauty of all literature. You discover that your longings are universal longings, that you're not lonely and isolated from anyone. You belong.*"

—F. SCOTT FITZGERALD

I remember reading a section of *War and Peace* and throwing it down, saying, "That's IT. That is EXACTLY how I feel!" No doubt you have had the same experience with another book.

It is so easy to feel out of place. To hold onto a story that we believe alienates us from other people. To create an "otherness" about ourselves or others that keeps us separate. What if we held onto a story of "I belong" and "other people feel this" instead?

Morning: No matter the situations you encounter today—whether in a business meeting or eating in a new restaurant—tell yourself "I belong" as your entry point. Start there.

Evening: What power does "I belong" have?

October 2

"He knew that any given thing on the face of the earth could reveal the history of all things. One could open a book to any page, or look at a person's hand; one could turn a card, or watch the flight of birds . . . whatever the thing observed, one could find a connection with his experience of the moment. Actually, it wasn't that those things, in themselves, revealed anything at all; it was just that people, looking at what was occurring around them, could find a means of penetration to the Soul of the World."

—PAULO COELHO

Today, see. Take a long look.

Morning: What is occurring around you today? Can you slow down enough to take a long look? Not just at the action, but at what is beneath the surface?

Evening: What if the answers you need could be discovered with a long look at what is?

October 3

Dorothy: Oh, will you help me? Can you help me?
Glinda the Good Witch: You don't need to be helped any longer.
You've always had the power to go back to Kansas.
Dorothy: I have?
Scarecrow: Then why didn't you tell her before?
Glinda the Good Witch: Because she wouldn't have
believed me. She had to learn it for herself.

—THE WIZARD OF OZ

The older I get, the more I recognize that *The Wizard of Oz* is a brilliant metaphor for life—that all we need to know about living is in that story.

One big a-ha for me when watching the film as an adult was that Dorothy had everything she needed inside herself all along. We all do. But in a world filled with the constant bombardment of messages that tell us we are broken or need help, we lose sight of our own internal knowing. It's time to reclaim that.

Morning: Today, anytime you feel unsure, remind yourself that you have everything you need inside yourself: "I have what I need. I just need to listen."

Evening: When you said, "I have what I need" to yourself today, how did that feel? Practice it over time and it will feel more grounded.

October 4

"*There comes a time in your life, when you walk away from all the drama and people who create it. You surround yourself with people who make you laugh. Forget the bad, and focus on the good. Love the people who treat you right, pray for the ones who don't. Life is too short to be anything but happy. Falling down is a part of life, getting back up is living.*"

—JOSÉ N. HARRIS

It's pretty simple—the quality of your life has nothing to do with other people or circumstances, and it has everything to do with your choice about how to *be* in that circumstance.

While I know people who are addicted to unhappiness, for most of us, happy is our choice. Whole industries have been built around finding happiness—but it's not something we find; it's something we create.

Morning: Do you usually choose happy? Watch what you choose today.

Evening: How can you remind yourself to choose happy tomorrow?

October 5

"Many people need desperately to receive this message: 'I feel and think much as you do, care about many of the things you care about, although most people do not care about them. You are not alone.'"

—KURT VONNEGUT

We hide our pain a lot, don't we? Until it becomes unbearable.

We believe we are the only person who feels that awful hurt, or is embarrassed by that failing, but we are not. We are most surely not.

No matter how small or sad you feel today, or tomorrow, or the next day, you are not alone.

Morning: Today, in your solitude, imagine yourself lifted up by all the others who feel the same aloneness. Imagine this kinship with every person you meet today—how does this change your interactions with them?

Evening: Community begins with the sharing of our stories—that's how we find commonalities, shared poverties, and the capacity for sisterhood. What story are you sharing?

October 6

"When I am constantly running there is no time for being. When there is no time for being there is no time for listening."

—MADELEINE L'ENGLE

You can't help others without first making sure you have your own needs met—like the flight attendants tell you about the oxygen masks on planes: Put yours on first before helping others. Because if you don't, you can't help others—you'll be unable to function.

What does putting your own mask on first look like to you? Does it look like slowing down and making time for just "being"? Does it look like taking the time to eat well or take a daily walk? Does it look like listening to your own body?

Morning: What self-care habit can you create, starting today?

Evening: What self-care habit will you commit to for the next thirty days?

October 7

"The essence of all beautiful art, all great art, is gratitude."

—FRIEDRICH NIETZSCHE

I met Kim Mailhot, the "Rock Fairy" who created these painted messages for *Your Daily Rock*, at a reading I did in Deerfield, New Hampshire, a few years ago. As I arrived, she was walking around the venue with a basket of painted rocks, inviting people to take one at random and contemplate the meaning of the message in their own lives.

Rock Fairies like Kim are amazing big-hearted people who create beauty and surprise and fling it into the world for others to find. Some rock fairies paint rocks, like Kim. Others write love letters to the sky and leave them in a public place for a stranger to find. Others leave a single flower on a park bench with a "cheer up" note. The possibilities are just endless.

Fling some beauty into the world today, with gratitude at its core.

Morning: How are you going to be a "rock fairy" today?

Evening: How can you show your gratitude for life tomorrow?

October 8

"Don't let the perfect be the enemy of the good."

—VOLTAIRE

Sometimes we need to lower the bar for ourselves. Not forever, but for a moment, to give ourselves a moment to breathe in the midst of all this striving.

Giving ourselves some grace is not failing, and it is not a deep dive into mediocrity either. You want to exercise thirty minutes a day, but never do? Set the bar at ten minutes a day and enjoy succeeding at it. You want to have friends over for dinner, but never have time to cook? Invite them over for take-out rather than miss the time to see them altogether. Allow yourself to have some "wins." Is that so hard?

This doesn't mean to "settle." It means to adapt to your true reality, not that ideal one that keeps us out of living.

Morning: How can you lower your standards today?

Evening: What is your first reaction to "lower your standards"? What can you learn from that reaction?

October 9

"In this sleepless night, as the darkness advances, look up at the sky and somehow remember that somewhere in this wide world, there are always people who love you, and people who need you. Because every person can't go on living alone."

—AI YAZAWA

A woman I knew through my work was found dead in her Las Vegas apartment a few years ago, a small pearl-handled pistol near her body. In her sleepless night, there was no sky, only suicide. If only she had remembered the stars and how they represented each one of us who knew her.

Remember. Remember that you are connected to others in ways you both know and don't know. Remember that you are loved.

Morning: Do you feel alone? Can you look to the stars for connection?

Evening: How can you feel less alone?

October 10

Be satisfied. Allow yourself to feel that unutterable fulfillment.
Want nothing.
How hard is that?

Morning: Try this on for size today: "I have everything I need." How does that feel?

Evening: How would believing that statement change your life?

October 11

carry a talisman.

> "The problem, often not discovered until late in life, is that when you look for things in life like love, meaning, motivation, it implies they are sitting behind a tree or under a rock. The most successful people in life recognize that in life they create their own love, they manufacture their own meaning, they generate their own motivation."

—NEIL DEGRASSE TYSON

Each of the objects we hold dear has a meaning to us that it holds for no one else. We imbue the things in our lives with a deeper sense of knowing—they represent something to us. A necklace represents young love, a pitcher we got for our first home represents far beyond its meaning as a vessel for pouring water. And it is true of what we carry around with us in this world, or should be. (Hint: Decluttering becomes easier if you shed the things without deeper meaning.)

Morning: What portable talisman or touchstone can you carry with you to remind you of what holds deep meaning in your life? A photograph? A small stone from a beach on which you feel most alive? Choose something to represent what you love and yearn for in your life. Carry it with you.

Evening: My talisman is the thing I touch in moments of panic or anger. Let yours become the same kind of comfort.

October 12

There is a time to be loud. And there is a time to be quiet. Never equate one with power and one with fear—that is a false assumption and one that perpetuates our need to be loud.

In fact, it is easy to be loud, and far harder to be quiet. And yet, when we whisper, people lean in to hear us.

Morning: Today, focus on your inside voice—inhabit silence and quietude.

Evening: In what ways is that more powerful than being loud?

October 13

"I wonder how much it would take to buy a soap bubble, if there were only one in the world."

—MARK TWAIN

I recently saw photographs of frozen bubbles made by a mom and her child one winter morning as they explored bubble-blowing in the cold. Gorgeous orbs reflecting the snow around them; beautiful even as they collapsed when the sun warmed them.

There is something freeing about bubbles—kids know this. The oil slicks of their surfaces, the way they rise, the element of not knowing when they will pop, the thrill of having one alight on our hand. Perhaps it is their ephemeral nature that makes them so special.

Morning: Adults need to blow bubbles too. Today, get some bubbles so you always have them on hand.

Evening: Before you go to bed, blow bubbles and watch what happens—to them, and to you.

October 14

Love without reservation.

"Nothing you become will disappoint me; I have no preconception that I'd like to see you be or do, I have no desire to forsee you, only to discover you. You can't disappoint me."

—MARY HASKELL

"Sure," the teenager said to me. "Sure, my mom believes in unconditional love, as long as I'm doing what she wants."

And here lies the challenge. It is easy to love when people are in line with what we believe to be true and right; less easy when they are making decisions that challenge us in some core way.

What if we adopted Mary Haskell's statement above as our belief system? That is what it means to love unconditionally, to love without reservation. Are we capable of this?

Morning: Write the Haskell quote on an index card and carry it with you. Read it until you have memorized it.

Evening: Now, in every encounter, with people you love, with people you don't know, with strangers on the street, recite that statement to yourself.

October 15

*"Haiku is not a shriek, a howl, a sigh, or a yawn;
rather, it is the deep breath of life."*

—SANTOKA TANEDA

I used to write book reviews in haiku. It was a beautiful chore, picking out five syllables for the first line, then seven for the second, then five for the last line. A challenge, indeed, to capture the gist of a book in seventeen syllables. The restriction wasn't limiting, but freeing, allowing me to get to the core of the book. For example, for *Middlesex* by Jeffrey Eugenides, I wrote:

> Are you boy or girl?
> We perform gender daily,
> each gesture, each look.

Haiku is the deep breath of life because it opens up clarity to us.

Morning: Following this form (five syllables, seven syllables, five syllables), capture your day in a series of haiku.

Evening: Read what you have written, and distill the day into one haiku. How is this final haiku the deep breath of this day?

October 16

"The purpose of art is washing the dust of daily life off our souls."

—PABLO PICASSO

As long as we separate "life" from "art," we will run up against the "I am not an artist" belief. This false story of separateness keeps us from being the artist of our own lives, the storyteller necessary for the story to be told, the one with the capacity to stop, and change the canvas into what we most want it to be.

If you're alive, you're creative. Why? Because every day, you are creating your life. It is not being done to you or for you—you are creating it yourself, with the decisions you make and don't make, with the choices you make about how to tell the story of your life. Don't abdicate that power to someone else.

Morning: Imagine your life so far as artwork on canvas. Describe or paint the painting.

Evening: Make this your mantra for tomorrow: "My life is a painting and a poem; I am the artist and the poet."

"Never shy away from opportunity and wholehearted living. Never be fearful of putting yourself out there. The courageous may encounter many disappointments, experience profound disillusionment, gather many wounds; but cherish your scars for they are the proud emblems of a truly phenomenal life. The fearful, cautious, cynical and self-repressed do not live at all. And that is simply no way to be in this world."

—ANTHON ST. MAARTEN

Does your heart have scars?
    Good. It means you are living fully.
    Carry on.

Morning: What scars do you proudly wear? Which do you hide, and why?

Evening: Of what are you fearful? How can you be more courageous, with your whole heart?

October 18

"There's a lot of difference between listening and hearing."

—G. K. CHESTERON

We get so many messages. From our bodies, from our surroundings, from our intuition, from our places of deepest knowing. We know. And yet we spend so much time denying that we know, denying that we need to reconsider or flee or embrace—whatever the message is, we shut it down. It's time to tune in to those messages. To hear, not merely listen.

What messages are you getting? About that volunteer opportunity or that new job—or about what your children are trying to tell you when they say, "Listen, Mama, listen!"

Where do you hear those messages in your body?

Morning: Today, listen to the messages. Really hear them. Heed them.

Evening: You've listened. Now hear.

October 19

"The book was turned to the page with Anne Frank's name, but what got me about it was the fact that right beneath her name there were four Aron Franks. FOUR. Four Aron Franks without museums, without historical markers, without anyone to mourn them. I silently resolved to remember and pray for the four Aron Franks as long as I was around."

—JOHN GREEN

I Googled my father years ago, and again last month. Nothing. He was born, lived, and died before the personal computer was created, let alone the Internet Machine. He had no followers or Facebook friends or retweets, and he never will. Melvin Lonnie Digh. Missing from the Internet. No museum, no historical marker. No page rankings. Just people who loved him and were loved by him, all left behind to remember him.

So many lives pass by, including our own at some point. Whom will you always remember and leave behind?

Morning: Tell a story today about someone you love who has died. Keep their name alive in that way.

Evening: Write one of your stories down to leave behind for others to remember.

October 20

*"You know that feeling you get when your leg falls asleep?
Well, I suddenly had that feeling in my spine. Like termites
were chewing through the marrow in my backbone."*

—NEAL SHUSTERMAN

What does "dread" mean?

1. To fear greatly; be in extreme apprehension of: *to dread death.*
2. to be reluctant to do, meet, or experience: *I dread going to big parties.*
3. *Archaic.* to hold in respectful awe.

We almost always remember those first two definitions, and almost never the third one.

What do you dread? Find a way to reframe it as something you are holding in respectful awe—how does that change things?

Morning: Make a list of three things you are dreading—a conversation with your ex? Making a speech? A medical test? Reframe those in terms of your respectful awe of them. What do you discover in doing so?

Evening: Remember this definition—to hold in respectful awe—for each time you feel "dread."

October 21

"Don't die with your music still inside you."

—WAYNE W. DYER

There is a full expression of who we are deep inside us—its expression is different for each of us. For some, it is a full measure of parenting, for others, a book or painting or a job well done. It might find expression as that moment when we give our child the last dinner roll, even though we wanted it for ourselves, or when we let someone into traffic ahead of us. Its expression need not be large, but simply and surely made.

Morning: What are you longing to "sing" with your life?

Evening: What music do you have in you that you want to let out? If you don't know, it's okay. Just open, open, and let fly what will.

October 22

"It is not the strongest or the most intelligent who will survive but those who can best manage change."

—CHARLES DARWIN

When we make big mistakes in the world, like denying the rights of human beings, I always think to myself, "Evolution is messy." We move forward, we stumble, we get fearful, we get eaten by lions, we revert to our little lizard selves, and then, maybe, we stand up again and move forward. It's messy, just like any change is messy, filled with both excitement and fear and this question: What are we losing?

How agile are you? Can you dance on this field of moving boulders we call life? What can you learn from the dance?

Morning: To wring our hands in dismay kicks us out of the process—stay in it today, say, "Evolution is messy," and step away from blame or wishing the boulders would stand still.

Evening: What is your pattern in terms of dealing with change? Is it a healthy one that serves you? If not, what can you do to change that?

October 23

"The best way to find out if you can trust somebody is to trust them."

—ERNEST HEMINGWAY

I trust people. Until I can no longer.

And even when that trust is breached, I immediately trust again.

It's just in my DNA. It keeps my heart and mind open. Do I get hurt? I do. Do I hurt others? I do. And I will be hurt and hurt again. But the alternative is far, far worse to me—living without trust, shutting down, making people prove themselves.

Who is in your circle of trust? People you trust and who trust you? Your go-to people. Who are they?

Morning: Name that circle of trust. Hold them and cherish them for the gifts they are.

Evening: Are you trustworthy?

October 24

"Everyone must leave something behind when he dies, my grandfather said. A child or a book or a painting or a house or a wall built or a pair of shoes made. Or a garden planted. Something your hand touched some way so your soul has somewhere to go when you die, and when people look at that tree or that flower you planted, you're there."

—RAY BRADBURY

Making our mark in this world, however big or small, means leaving behind a touchstone.

What are you leaving behind?

Morning: Make a list of what you are leaving behind.

Evening: What would you like to leave behind?

October 25

"You are one of a kind. You are lucky enough to have something that makes you different from everyone else. Embrace your individuality. Self-worth comes from one thing: thinking you are worthy. So appreciate what it feels like underneath your own skin; you are amazing just the way you are."

—MELCHOR LIM

In my upbringing, it was not okay to say, "I am fantastic!" because that was boastful. There didn't seem to be a difference between healthy self-esteem and boastfulness; there was no room for either one. It wasn't Godly, it appears.

While I felt supported by family in almost all that I did, it wasn't for me to mention my accomplishments, but for them to be noticed by others. That's just how it was.

So acknowledging my uniqueness and gifts has a lot of baggage attached to it for me.

Morning: How about you? What were your messages growing up about your uniqueness and talents?

Evening: Is it hard for you to say, "I am amazing just the way I am"? Practice.

October 26

"Of course, I have given my engineers some headaches over the years,
but they go with me. I have always wanted my buildings to be as light as
possible, to touch the ground gently, to swoop and soar, and to surprise."

—OSCAR NIEMEYER

I love the thought that Niemeyer's architecture is a symbol for what we can also wish for our hearts—as light as possible, to touch the ground gently, to swoop and soar, and to surprise.

If we construct our heart's passage through life with those design elements, we will surely find in the building of it what makes it soar, what makes it fall, what makes it soar.

Morning: Imagine you are crafting a building with your heart—describe the building you wish to build.

Evening: What tools are you missing to create that building?

"Time goes, you say? Ah no! Alas, Time stays, we go."

—HENRY AUSTIN DOBSON

We believe time is fleeting, but we are, instead.

Either way, our time here is short, shorter, shortest. So short, too quickly gone. And yet we waste our days in so many ways.

Because time is short, awaken each morning to a new life, one day long. See what rainbow of emotions and sensations you can fit into that life, that day, and then, come sunset, let go of that day.

Morning: Today is a new life, lasting only this one day. What do you most long for it to contain?

Evening: How will you honor and let go of this day?

October 28

"There is no greatness where there is not simplicity, goodness, and truth."

—LEO TOLSTOY

We don't trust simple because we believe it needs to be more . . . complicated. That simplicity is for the simple-minded.

But often, simple is the thing that works. Like a baseball player whose batting average slumps, prompting every possible medical and psychological test in the book—until one day he mentions that his feet hurt, and it is discovered that his shoes are too tight. Larger shoe = better batting average. Problem solved in the simplest way possible.

Morning: Trust the simple. Look for it first.

Evening: What challenges are you facing now? List a few, and then brainstorm simple solutions.

October 29

"But I suppose the most revolutionary act one can engage in is . . . to tell the truth."

—HOWARD ZINN

I think most of us would be willing to tell our truth . . . if we only knew what our truth was.

How can we know? Not by merely thinking about it until it emerges fully formed from our foreheads, but by also allowing ourselves to acknowledge and give weight to how we feel, sense, intuit the world around us. We can only know our truth, sometimes, in relationship to untruth, in close proximity to what we don't believe. Sometimes we can only know it in a "yes" that immediately feels like it should have been a "no" instead.

Your truth is an active verb. You have to feel it, experiment with it, put it out in the field to look at it from a distance sometimes before you can speak it.

Morning: What is your truth? What do you know about it? What don't you know? What boundaries or horizons does your truth close down or open up?

Evening: Can you tell your (not "the") absolute truth for one day?

October 30

"You can't connect the dots looking forward; you can only connect them looking backwards. So you have to trust that the dots will somehow connect in your future. You have to trust in something— your gut, destiny, life, karma, whatever. This approach has never let me down, and it has made all the difference in my life."

—STEVE JOBS

As a child, I loved connect-the-dots pictures (I still do). The anticipation! Once you get past the obvious ones where the dots are huge and few, showing easily the outline of a giraffe, the suspense is wonderful—what will it be? With your No. 2 pencil, you trace from 1 to 2 and beyond, waiting for the moment when you can say, "It's a tree!" or, "It's an elephant!"

In life, we are also connecting the dots, always. One moment connects to another and another, and it is only when we get to the last dot that we can look back and say, "It's my life!"

Morning: Are you living forward or backward? Trust that the dots will connect in your future and carry on.

Evening: We see patterns after we've lived them, not before. Because before all we can see is the living, not the ways in which grooves are being created over time. Those dots. We're connecting them all the time—we just can't see them.

October 31

Find meaning in the space we call November, these thirty days of life we will never live again.

As Jennifer Egan wrote in *A Visit from the Goon Squad*, "'Sure, everything is ending,' Jules said, 'but not yet.'" Don't be living so much into the New Year that you lose the last two months of this one.

And, conversely, as the Navajo say, "Don't let yesterday use up too much of today."

November

Make peace with these conditions.

"We can never obtain peace in the outer world until we make peace with ourselves."

—DALAI LAMA

I used to work with a woman who was really smart but had a hard time expressing herself. She would often say things like, "Isn't that incredible?" and I could never tell if she meant it was incredibly good or incredibly bad. Just so, life itself poses the same challenges. "Isn't it incredible?" rests entirely with our interpretation.

Morning: When you find yourself reacting to something that happens in your external environment today—a downpour as you are walking back from lunch without your umbrella, news of another economic downturn, a sorrowful phone call—pause. Remember to create peace inside yourself first, in order to make peace with what is outside you.

Evening: Is your mind peaceful? Your heart?

November 1

"He might have been naive, but he didn't care; he said he's rather die with his heart on his sleeve than end up another cynic."

—COLUM MCCANN

I love being naive. It might be one of my best traits.

Some people call it being a Pollyanna. Some people call it being stupid. If that's true, it's a very happy stupid Pollyanna that I am, then.

Is it naive to assume positive intent in all situations? Some might think so. I think it is raising the level of dialogue and hopefulness to what we long for life to be—more full of awe and joy and trust.

Morning: Don't protect yourself from awe today. Let yourself feel it fully. Don't worry about looking naive. Naive = childlike = fantastic. Get outside. Every single thing out there will fill you with awe. If you let it.

Evening: Remind yourself tomorrow to assume positive intent in every situation—in that, you will find awe. For example: Someone cut you off? They must have had an emergency situation and been panicked about something. See? It doesn't cost you anything to reframe. Is it true? Does it matter?

November 2

"She had never imagined she had the power to make someone else so happy. And not a magical power, either—a purely human one."

What purely human powers do you have?
    Don't immediately say, "None." Think about it.

    You have the power to say yes and say no.
    You have the power to be a good friend, or not.
    You have the power to ask for the kind of help you
    need.
    You have the power to help yourself.

    The list is endless, you magical human.

Morning: Today, make note of the purely human powers you often overlook. Use them well.

Evening: What powers did you discover you have today?

November 3

*"Letter writing is the only device for combining
solitude with good company."*

—LORD BYRON

I grew up in the age of pen pals, when letters from across the
country or from around the world took their own sweet time
making their way to you, tucked into the deep leather bag of a
letter carrier. Oh, the sight of all those stamps and handwriting.

Oh, pen. Oh, paper. I've missed you so. Handwriting is
such a beautiful way we can own language.

In our digital world, a handwritten note becomes more sym-
bolic of an act of thoughtfulness and caring; it is a beautiful act
of deliberateness. The feel of the paper, the choice of the pen,
the sealing of the envelope, that stamp—personal, intentional,
loving. Then the added emphasis that comes with being able to
scribble or doodle to add emphasis; a handwritten "xoxo" holds
so much more love and potential. The scent of you from where
you sit by the window writing, transmitted to the one you love
far away. The fact that you touched it.

All this.

Morning: Have a conversation with someone today in your own
handwriting. And mail it to them.

Evening: Create a small space in your house for stationery,
pens, and stamps. Make letter-writing a habit of love.

November 4

"I love you without knowing how, or when, or from where. I love you simply, without problems or pride: I love you in this way because I do not know any other way of loving but this, in which there is no I or you, so intimate that your hand upon my chest is my hand, so intimate that when I fall asleep your eyes close."

—PABLO NERUDA

There is a long legacy of "anyway"—as in, we only live so long so why should we be concerned about long-range projects that will outlast us. But while the library we build will be dismantled, we build it anyway; the books we read will be forgotten over time, but we read them anyway. The people we help may neglect us or forget the help, but we help people anyway.

Continue the legacy of "anyway." It is a legacy that helps us be fully human.

Morning: What do you do "anyway"? Pay attention to this question today.

Evening: What is unconditional love to you? That's what "anyway" is all about.

November 5

"I hated myself for going, why couldn't I be the kind of person who stays?"

—JONATHAN SAFRAN FOER

When I was in my first real job, the CEO asked me to attend a meeting of all his direct reports. He was new to the organization and wanted to set the tone for all the department heads.

But I wasn't a department head—I was someone who just happened to report to him, but without a department. I went. After the first hour the CEO said he wanted to talk about the performance review system after the break.

I excused myself and left the meeting, since I assumed he didn't mean me. The next day, he called me into his office to ask why I wasn't there. I explained my reasoning. "Patti," he said, "never take yourself out of the picture. Make someone else take you out. Assume you are needed until you are told you're not."

Morning: Today, don't let your stories of yourself take you out of the picture. Take a seat until someone asks you to leave.

Evening: What story are you telling yourself about your place in the world?

November 6

Flip the question.

"Judge a man by his questions rather than by his answers."

—VOLTAIRE

My friend Eliav Zakay leads a national youth leadership development program. As part of the two-year training for fifteen- to seventeen-year-olds, they work in teams on a community project.

One young team started their project with this question: "How can our community better serve people with mental retardation?" They worked on the question for a while, without satisfying results. Then one day, they flipped the question to this: "How can our people with mental retardation better serve the community?"

The lightbulbs went on. With that change, a dynamic, sustainable, empowering project was created in which the students taught leadership skills to people with mental retardation who then went into the community with social service projects of their own—for example, a food drive for people without the means to afford a holiday meal, serving a need and feeling great about themselves as needed parts of the community as well.

Morning: What question have you been asking, without results? How can you flip that question today?

Evening: This is a powerful tool. What other questions can you flip?

November 7

"You will be your best self when you take time to understand what you really need, feel and want."

—DEBORAH DAY

What do you really need?

What do you really feel?

What do you really want?

These are three powerful questions to ask yourself today. And they are a necessary prerequisite to making your needs known—first you need to know. Sometimes, often, we skip that step and then wonder why we're not getting what we really need and want.

Morning: Focus on one question today: What do you really need? Not want, but need?

Evening: Move on to the other two questions: What do you really feel? Not what you think you should feel. And what do you really want? Not what your parents want for you or what society wants for you.

November 8

Let go of the old story.

"The greater part of human pain is unnecessary. It is self-created as long as the unobserved mind runs your life."

—ECKHART TOLLE

An expert in rare and antiquarian books, my husband, John, is often invited to appraise people's book collections. And sometimes he has to wander through homes filled with old newspapers and magazines, piled so high he has to follow a small path between them. Like *Hoarders*, but pre–reality TV.

"Newspapers from the morning are really no longer even relevant by the same afternoon," he told me after once such visit. "So it's really striking to go into someone's house and see decades' worth of newspapers waiting to be read and clipped."

So much weight, so much space taken up by old news, old stories. What is the weight of your old stories? Were you always described as temperamental as a child, so are hanging on to that story as an adult? You have the option to let go of those old stories, and clear a path for new ones.

Morning: Write as many answers to this as you can: "I am
_____." For example, "I am a CEO. I am an only child. I am on antidepressants. I am sure I'm not worthy." Dive as deeply as you can. Sit with that list today.

Evening: Review that list—how many definitions of who you are might no longer be true? Which ones do you want to let go?

November 9

"I hope that while so many people are out smelling the flowers, someone is taking the time to plant some."

—HERBERT RAPPAPORT

I'm a self-conscious gardener. I don't really know what I'm doing, but I try. Oh lord, I try.

So while there are many things I don't understand about gardening, I do know that many plants require regular care in order to bloom or produce vegetables. That is, once the planting is done, our work needs to continue. And each plant has his or her own needs.

So, too, with love—it needs nurturing over time in order to bloom. And peace can't bloom without seeds of love. It's an important task, this garden of our lives.

Morning: What are you planting?

Evening: What do you hope to harvest?

November 10

"If your heart is broken, make art with the pieces."

—SHANE KOYCZAN

Being unstoppable doesn't mean never stopping. It means pausing when you need to in order to catch your breath. It means taking the time you need. It means making art with the pieces of your broken heart rather than throwing them away or hiding them away. It means singing when you want to, not when people say it's good or worthy.

Being unstoppable doesn't mean you have to be Superwoman. It means you carry on, carry on. You stand back up, after taking the break you need to notice what is around you when you're down—and that you pick something up from the ground to bring back with you.

Being unstoppable means you carry on.

Morning: Carry on.

Evening: What heartache can you make art with today? Tomorrow?

November 11

*"While you are alive collect moments not things, earn
respect not money and enjoy love not luxuries."*

—AARTI KHURANA

If you were to put under your bed a salvage box of things that
you would carry out of your house were it to catch on fire, what
would those objects be? My guess is that most of the objects
would be photographs—the holders of memory that could easily
excite us to remember more. The other bits would probably be
seemingly insignificant talismans to prompt memories as well.

When we downsized last year, we did so to focus on moments,
experiences, and love. It is the best, most freeing, most significant move we have ever made. There is a freedom in focusing
on moments. They don't need to be dusted, for one thing.

In the end, it is the collection of memory that is of the highest importance to us—the recollection of moments, not things.

Morning: What would be in your box? Get a box and start fill-
ing it.

Evening: Are you collecting moments, respect, and love? Or
are you collecting things, money, and luxuries?

November 12

"From the writer's perspective, audience is always an act of the imagination."

—BILLY MARSHALL STONEKING

In a memoir class a few years ago, a young woman was writing a very hot story about a love affair she once had. As she read from the piece each week for our workshop, people started fanning themselves—and yet she wasn't writing about sex. "Write the sex scene," our teacher told her. She blushed, and the rest of us started having hot flashes at the very idea of it.

"I couldn't do that!" she said. "I could never do that. What if my parents read that?"

"Write it, and then delete it. But you need to write it because the act of writing it will get you to another place and a deeper understanding of your story."

The act of writing the unmentionable tells us what the story really is. Sometimes we have to write like an orphan, with no thought of the audience, in order to get there.

Morning: Write what you really long to write. Then eat it, burn it, delete it. It is the writing that will take you to different place in that story.

Evening: How does this advice apply to the rest of your life?

November 13

Make fear your Companion.

"We can easily forgive a child for being afraid of the dark; the real tragedy of life is when people are afraid of the light."

—PLATO

What does fear achieve in our lives?

> It shuts us down.
> It makes us smaller.
> It is reductive, not generative.
> It makes us live from a place of protection rather than exploration.
> It becomes larger the more we resist it.
> It can sometimes save our life.

Let's befriend fear rather than demonize it. The first step in that process is to acknowledge the fear, then greet it, then spend time with it, then keep in touch with it over time, then be there for it when it needs you. Just like a friendship.

Morning: What do you fear? Make as complete a list as you can: "I fear snakes. I fear something happening to my children. I fear dementia. I fear being irrelevant. I fear . . ."

Evening: For each fear you've listed, and thinking of the stages of making a friend that you know in your life, how can you befriend these fears?

November 14

"Passion is the source of our finest moments. The joy of love . . . the clarity of hatred . . . the ecstasy of grief. It hurts sometimes more than we can bear. If we could live without passion, maybe we'd know some kind of peace. But we would be hollow. Empty rooms, shuttered and dank. Without passion, we'd be truly dead."

—JOSS WHEDON

A few years ago, as a museum guard watched a young girl approach a painting, he readied himself to tell her not to touch it. Then he realized that she had her tongue out and was about to lick the blue velvet skirt of the woman in the painting. "Please don't lick the art!" he shouted out to her to get her to stop, a phrase now found on T-shirts in the museum gift shop.

Oh, how she must have loved and wanted to wholly experience that blue velvet skirt.

Do you let yourself feel that kind of fire?

Morning: What are you on fire about in your life?

Evening: How does a wood fire get ignited? What can you learn from that process to ignite a fire in your life?

November 15

"History will be kind to me because I intend to write it."

—WINSTON CHURCHILL

There are many crests and family shields that employ the phrase (in whatever language) "Take Action," or "Do," or "Diligence," or some derivative of an active verb. (This is why I named my book, *Life Is a Verb* rather than *Life Is an Adverb* or *Noun* or *Adjective*)

The family crest using a motto of "Sit Still" or "Wait for a Time that Is More Convenient" doesn't find too many takers.

Morning: What is your motto, in six words or less? What would be on your bumper sticker (the modern equivalent of a family crest)?

Evening: How can you live into that motto?

November 16

"We are all travelers in the wilderness of this world, and the best we can find in our travels is an honest friend."

—ROBERT LOUIS STEVENSON

I like watching *The X Factor* because of the strong offers being made by people auditioning. And just as much, I love watching the judges giving their feedback. The person everyone waits to hear from is Simon Cowell. Why? Because they know he will tell the truth, no matter how hard it is to hear. And sometimes he isn't very kind about it, but sometimes he deeply is.

A preacher, too large to stand at 540 pounds, once auditioned from his wheelchair. Simon liked his voice, and in a quiet response, said, "You know this is on you, don't you? I will support you if you will support yourself and do the work you need to do." It was a moment of true kindness, and true honesty.

Morning: Can you marry honesty with kindness instead of looking at them as an either/or equation? What is gained by doing so?

Evening: What other either/or beliefs can you shift into both/and equations instead?

November 17

"So my antagonist said, 'Is it impossible that there are flying saucers? Can you prove that it's impossible?' 'No,' I said, 'I can't prove it's impossible. It's just very unlikely.' At that he said, 'You are very unscientific. If you can't prove it impossible then how can you say that it's unlikely?' But that is the way that is scientific. It is scientific only to say what is more likely and what less likely, and not to be proving all the time the possible and impossible."

—RICHARD P. FEYNMAN

If you take away "baby," nobody would disagree that "steps count."

If you redefine "baby" as "small" or "successive" or "incremental" or "thoughtful," then you're starting to describe a scientific process. And in doing science the big ideas are great, yes, but the importance is made in the details, in the small and careful increments—in the baby steps.

Morning: What baby steps can you take today?

Evening: Were you able to take those steps without discounting them by saying they are too small?

"Anger and fear can turn you into a different person. They mask what you're really feeling, and they allow you to destroy something that doesn't deserve it, something that should be cared for and protected."

—NATALIE WARD

In *The Expression of the Emotions in Man and Animals*, Charles Darwin noted the similarity of expression in different emotions, noting that trembling can be an expression of fear, or rage, or joy.

Our daughter Tess, like many children with Asperger's syndrome, is prone to meltdowns on a grand scale. We used to say, "How can such a small child feel such rage?" Until our friend Catherine suggested from her experience with clients with Asperger's that what Tess was feeling wasn't rage, but panic.

Morning: When you see an angry person, consider them fearful. See if that changes your response to them.

Evening: What do you do when you're feeling panicked? Do you disappear? Lash out? What might your actions look like to someone else?

November 19

And let us not forget: Human are animals too, soft and huggy.

"Huggy" might mean something different for people in your life—perhaps they aren't huggers, but talkers or laughers. Meet them where they are to show love in a way they can understand.

Morning: Show some love today with a "hug" or two.

Evening: What keeps you from showing love to others?

November 20

"Do something every day that is loving toward your body and gives you the opportunity to enjoy the sensations of your body."

—GOLDA PORETSKY

We extend a lot of energy outside ourselves. We have a lot of responsibilities.

Can we redirect some of that energy toward ourselves, instead? Not to be selfish, but to be whole, filled up enough to take care of others without resentment or exhaustion?

We need to restore ourselves.

Morning: What one thing will you do today that is loving toward your body?

Evening: What did you do, and how did it feel? What will you do tomorrow to nurture yourself? This is a daily practice.

November 21

"If you think you can do a thing or think you can't do a thing, you're right."

—HENRY FORD

Trapeze class.

They tried to teach me how to pull my legs up over the bar in midair in order to fling myself toward the other flyer who was reaching out to me. "I'm too heavy to do this," "I don't have the ab muscles for this," "I'm so afraid of heights," "I look ridiculous."

Atop the platform, I expressed all this to the young man who would kick me off into the air if I couldn't bring myself to do it. "The only thing stopping you from doing this is right here," he said, pointing to his head. And then he kicked me into the air where I failed, unable to tell where I was in space.

The difference between "can" and "can't" is the width of one "t" and a little piece of punctuation that really doesn't want to be there.

Morning: What are you telling yourself you can't do? Make a list.

Evening: What is the block to each of those things on the list?

November 22

"If you lose direction, go to a higher ground."

—TOBA BETA

The animals in the 2004 Asian tsunami were the first to know. What did they do? They moved to higher ground in an event that killed nearly 250,000 people in fourteen nations.

We get lost. We are endangered sometimes. We have to be able to trust our animal instinct, just as those animals did. We need to get to higher ground in order to see, and see clearly.

Physicist Hermann von Helmholtz wrote about the "royal road," that straight line we can see from the top of the mountain to where we started our journey. That line isn't straight when we're climbing—far from it. We can only see that straight path from the top.

When in doubt, or when lost, seek higher ground to see more clearly.

Morning: What in your life do you need a different perspective on?

Evening: What keeps you from following your "gut" instinct?

November 23

"We hand one another along."

—WALKER PERCY

In his novel *The Moviegoer*, Walker Percy writes that we hand one another along, a beautiful way of stating our interdependence and responsibilities as humans to one another. Ram Dass has put this another, also memorable, way: "We're all just walking each other home."

Each invokes the image of a journey, of a passage we all take. Who is walking you home? Whom are you walking home? Whose hand are you holding in order to hand them along?

Morning: We have all been handed along—who has supported you in that way in your life? Have you said "thank you" to them?

Evening: What does "just walking each other home" mean to you? Can you be counted on to do that?

November 24

*"We are each of us angels with only one wing, and
we can only fly by embracing one another."*

—LUCIANO DE CRESCENZO

Here is something I know for sure: We can never know what
angels surround us. It is a leap of faith to consider all the
humans (and animals) we encounter as angels—but great, and
sometimes simple and beautiful, things happen when we do.

Morning: Look around you at all the angels.

Evening: Whose angel are you? What if you considered yourself
the angel of everyone you meet? How might that change your
encounters?

November 25

"It is the nature of grace always to fill spaces that have been empty."

—JOHANN WOLFGANG VON GOETHE

I am unsure if I fully understand what grace is and does. I know how it feels, though. It feels like a supportive arm, helping me back up after I tumble. It feels like a hug that fills me up, that pressing of body against another, the relaxation of that boundary. It feels like mercy.

Grace is opening possibility for myself and others; it is seeing "failures" as precious; it is allowing me to lower my bar and it fills spaces that have been empty in such a rich, whole way. Not with junk food, but with a gourmet meal. That's how grace feels.

Morning: How does grace feel to you?

Evening: Can you let grace fill up your empty spaces?

November 26

"Thirty-nine years of my life had passed before I understood that clouds were not my enemy; that they were beautiful, and that I needed them. I suppose this, for me, marked the beginning of wisdom. Life is short."

—IIMANI DAVID

We've had big thunderstorms every afternoon this week—buckets of rain and loud thunder and wind, driving all of us to one bed where I read aloud to keep Tess feeling safe.

When the rain and storms come, it is easy to blame the clouds—sometimes we even begin to assign maliciousness to the sky when we see the darkening.

Can we thank them for the color instead?

Morning: What color can you thank your "clouds" for today?

Evening: Reframe, reframe, reframe. It saves lives; it makes the darkness beautiful, and necessary.

November 27

"You can pretend to care, but you can't pretend to show up."

—AMY MCCRACKEN

Amy shows up like no one else—she helped save John's life when he was diagnosed with kidney cancer by raising money to pay for life-saving tests and surgery. She runs marathons to fight blood cancers, does extreme hikes to fight cystic fibrosis, and much more.

Fundraising is her gift—what's yours? There are so many ways we can show up.

Morning: How can you show up today?

Evening: How do you like for others to show up for you? For some of us, it is physical presence; for others, a phone call or note in the mail. How can people know, unless you tell them? How can you know how to show up for others, unless you ask them?

November 28

"'No way, man. I got one rule as a driver.' 'What's that?' 'Never look in da rearview mirror.' 'Never?' We drifted into the left-hand lane, cutting off a cab. 'It's not healthy to keep a' watchin' what you leavin' behind.'"

—MARISHA PESSL

We spend a lot of today thinking about yesterday—what we should have done, what we ought to have done differently. But the view in the rearview mirror not only is tiny but takes our view off the road ahead.

Leave it; look ahead.

Morning: Don't let yesterday take up too much of today, says an old Navajo saying. When you feel yourself looking back with regret, find a way to turn your eyes back to the road ahead— before you hit that cab.

Evening: Hindsight gives a look at boundaries, things not done or done; looking forward gives us a look at horizons. What horizons are you driving toward?

November 29

"He leans over and takes her hand. With the other he touches her face. 'You your best thing, Sethe. You are.' His holding fingers are holding hers. 'Me? Me?'"

—TONI MORRISON

It is beautiful to have someone say they love us, that we are the best thing. Even if we don't quite believe it.

But the real joy in life comes when we choose to love ourselves. Then we are unstoppable, full, more able to love others.

What does loving yourself look like in your life?

What does not loving yourself look like in your life?

Morning: How will you show yourself that you love who you are today?

Evening: What keeps you from loving yourself? Can you lower that bar?

November 30

The last thirty-one days of this year.

How on earth did it speed by so quickly? Even when we are paying close attention and being mindful of each day, it moves on with impressive speed.

And yet.

And yet, when we are focused on each day, the passing matters less than this moment, right now. It is a constant tension we feel between stasis and speed. And in such a way, we spend our lives.

December

"If only it were that easy to let go of hate. Just relax your face."

—LAINI TAYLOR

There is a softening that happens when we are in love, when we have survived a treacherous moment, that time after knowing something fierce and big. We soften, sometimes because we have learned how softening changes our life and makes us more vulnerable and real, and sometimes because we have lost control of all those muscles that harden us.

What if we just focused on our faces today? On relaxing our faces so they are soft and open and inviting?

Morning: Relax your face consciously today. Set an alarm for every hour, and when it rings, allow your face to relax. Tighten it, then relax it, and repeat. Feel the softening.

Evening: What was your experience of softening today?

December 1

"Even the wildest dreams have to start somewhere. Allow yourself the time and space to let your mind wander and your imagination fly."

—OPRAH WINFREY

Our lives, when we add them all up at the end, are the sum of our deepest yearnings meeting the challenges we call obstacles.

We want our lives to have more meaning, and we feel that doing laundry gets in the way.

We want to love and be loved, and we feel that needing to protect ourselves gets in the way.

We yearn for peace, for significance, for success—whatever it is we yearn for—and our journey is thwarted, we feel.

But those obstacles are our teachers, placed along that path to teach us, if we can sit with them, know them, walk hand in hand with them. These obstacles *are* our lives.

Let yourself yearn. Give voice to your deepest dream. And remember, always, that the dream isn't the point. The journey is where the magic is.

Morning: What are your wildest dreams for your life?

Evening: What do you believe is standing in your way? Do you let those obstacles reduce your dream?

December 2

"One day you meet someone and for some inexplicable reason, you feel more connected to this stranger than anyone else—closer to them than your closest family. Perhaps this person carries within them an angel—one sent to you for some higher purpose; to teach you an important lesson or to keep you safe during a perilous time. What you must do is trust in them—even if they come hand in hand with pain or suffering—the reason for their presence will become clear in due time."

—LANG LEAV

What if everyone you meet today is an angel, sent especially to you? Would that change how you met the world today? Would that alter your interactions with people you know and don't know?

Consider it so.

Morning: This is your charge today—to trust the angels around you. To see everyone as your angel.

Evening: How did this change you, and change your day?

December 3

"There are two basic motivating forces: fear and love. When we are afraid, we pull back from life. When we are in love, we open to all that life has to offer with passion, excitement, and acceptance. We need to learn to love ourselves first, in all our glory and our imperfections. If we cannot love ourselves, we cannot fully open to our ability to love others or our potential to create. Evolution and all hopes for a better world rest in the fearlessness and open-hearted vision of people who embrace life."

—JOHN LENNON

Let love evaporate your fear. Open up rather than pulling back.

Morning: Think of fear as a constriction of your heart muscle, and love an opening up of the flow from it. Today, consciously think of your heart in that way. Both are necessary for life, that constriction and that flow, aren't they?

Evening: How can you be more fearless in your life? By loving more. Try this.

December 4

"In a room where people unanimously maintain a conspiracy of silence, one word of truth sounds like a pistol shot."

—CZESLAW MILOSZ

Witnessing, in the sense of full participation and investment in the process, is a beautiful thing. We are witnesses at weddings, for example, playing not a passive but an active role in the construct of that ritual.

Likewise, when we are witnesses to injustice or violence, or simple human unkindness, we are also playing an active role and making choices: to be silent, or to speak up. Choose to speak up.

(And when you speak truth, remember that you can only "tell it like it is" for you. Other people's "like it is" will be different, their truths individual. Don't let this dissuade you from breaking the silence.)

Morning: Just notice what you witness, but don't speak up about today. Notice without judging yourself for remaining silent.

Evening: For each of the moments when you remained silent today, draft a few sentences about what you wish your response had been. Read them aloud. Remember them for the next time. Telling it like it is isn't easy sometimes. Practice will help.

December 5

*"Progress means getting nearer to the place you want to be. And if
you have taken a wrong turning, then to go forward does not get
you any nearer. If you are on the wrong road, progress means doing
an about-turn and walking back to the right road; and in that case
the man who turns back soonest is the most progressive man."*

—C. S. LEWIS

Yes, look how far you've come.

More importantly, make sure you are on the right road.

Morning: Pause in your journey before going farther. Change
direction if you need to.

Evening: Remember: Turning around is a valid choice, no
matter how far you've already come.

December 6

"Simply being with someone is difficult because it asks of us that we share in the other's vulnerability, enter with him or her into the experience of weakness and powerlessness, become part of the uncertainty, and give up control and self-determination."

—HENRI J. M. NOUWEN

We surprise people with presents all the time; with presence, less so.

Be willing to simply be present with someone who is in pain, without expectation of anything but your presence. You might find it more difficult than deflecting with a potted plant or Hallmark card, but far more meaningful.

Morning: Who needs the simple but powerful gift of your presence?

Evening: How can you shift your perspective from presents to presence?

December 7

know it will end.

"There's a trick to the 'graceful exit.' It begins with the vision to recognize when a job, a life stage, or a relationship is over—and let it go. It means leaving what's over without denying its validity or its past importance to our lives. It involves a sense of future, a belief that every exit line is an entry, that we are moving up, rather than out."

—ELLEN GOODMAN

If there is a truth, it is this: Everything ends.

Mostly, we avoid that truth, or deny it. We fight to make it not so. We grab on tighter, we kick and scream about unfairness. We lose sight of what was good when it is gone. We anticipate endings by steeling ourselves against them. We don't go peaceful into that good night.

But what if endings were grace notes? What if endings were the only thing that moved us forward? One of Buddha's questions for us to ask at the end of our lives is, "Did I let go deeply?"

Morning: Do you let go deeply? Or do you resist endings? What might change if instead of resisting, you befriended the end?

Evening: Can you leave what is over without invalidating what was?

December 8

be
someone's
lighthouse.

"The dip of the light meant that the island itself was always left in darkness. A lighthouse is for others; powerless to illuminate the space closest to it."

—M. L. STEDMAN

My friend Kim sat me down six months ago and said, "I'm worried that this business partnership is not good for you." We talked for hours and hours. And she was right.

Just like that, lighthouses warn of danger. And because we can be lighthouses for others and not ourselves—the light we have can't illuminate the land right around us, it seems—we need friends who can be lighthouses for us.

Too often, though, even if we see danger, we don't say so because we're not sure of the complexity of the situation or how the warnings will be received. But it's not the job of the lighthouse to steer the ship, is it? It is there to be constant and steady and shed light.

Morning: Whose lighthouse can you be?

Evening: Can you let someone in enough to be your lighthouse?

December 9

I love odd things. Quirky, interesting, oddball things. Like buildings shaped like flowerpots or a monument to twine. These things make me happy.

Almost none of these things are on the highway. The highway is for speed, not interest. Sometimes the highway is required—getting there quickly. And sometimes the back roads are required—enjoying the journey.

This is, of course, a metaphor for life.

Morning: Take the back roads today. See what you see.

Evening: How hard is it for you to slow down?

December 10

"We only have what we give."

—ISABEL ALLENDE

Do you appreciate the opportunity to help other people? Most of us do.

Yet most of us are hesitant to ask for help: We don't want to be a burden or appear weak.

When you help others, do you think they are a burden or weak? No, you are glad to be of assistance. We all are. So why do we create that story for ourselves? Why do we stop the flow of helpfulness?

Other people don't know what you need unless you communicate it. By allowing others to help you, it does not mean you are weak. It means you are strong enough to reach out. Don't stop reaching out.

Morning: Ask someone for help today. Be open for them to say "yes" or "no." Their response is less important than your asking.

Evening: How did that feel?

December 11

"It is a common belief that we breathe with our lungs alone, but in point of fact, the work of breathing is done by the whole body. The lungs play a passive role in the respiratory process."

—ALEXANDER LOWEN

First, we need to stop.

Second, we need to breathe with our whole body, not just our lungs.

Third, we need to repeat this throughout our days.

What does breathing provide you?

Your life.

Respect it more than you have been.

Morning: Show breathing your respect today.

Evening: Can you dedicate five minutes to paying attention to your breathing today?

December 12

"For the dead and the living, we must bear witness."

—ELIE WIESEL

So much of life just needs to be seen. So many of us wish for nothing more than to be seen. No fix is necessary, though that is where we go first: "I can fix this for you."

I used to facilitate a nine-week dialogue on black/white racism in Asheville, North Carolina. Without fail, by the second week a white man would stand up with a marker and start planning how to fix racism in our community. "This cannot stand," he would say. "We've got to do something about this." There would be a pause, and then one of the African-American members of the group would say, "But you haven't even heard our story yet."

What if we let go of fixing, and simply bear witness? It calls on a deeper self than the one raised to solve problems—it means we have to go beyond seeing problems to embrace the core verb: "to be."

Morning: When is the last time you simply let yourself be with someone? When you feel drawn to "fixing" today, step away and into simply being.

Evening: What part of yourself is engaged when you are fixing? What part of yourself is engaged when you are bearing witness?

December 13

> "Look at your feet. You are standing in the sky. When we think of the sky, we tend to look up, but the sky actually begins at the earth. We walk through it, yell into it, rake leaves, wash the dog, and drive cars in it. We breathe it deep within us. With every breath, we inhale millions of molecules of sky, heat them briefly, and then exhale them back into the world."

—DIANE ACKERMAN

In a writing class I teach online, I ask participants to write a love letter to the sky and leave it somewhere for a stranger to find. I love the idea of finding a paean to the sky at the park, or in the parking lot, or library, or in the frozen-food section at the grocery store.

Look at the sky. You are holding it up, and it is holding you up, pressing against you. You are inhaling sky—what is your relationship with it?

Morning: Write a love letter to the sky and leave it somewhere for a stranger to find today.

Evening: How does "sky" change when you see it in the way Diane Ackerman suggests rather than "looking up" at it?

December 14

"Accept applause, sure, please do. But when you expect applause, when you do your work in order (and because of) applause, you have sold yourself short. That's because your work is depending on something out of your control."

—SETH GODIN

Accept, but don't expect, applause.

And by accept, I mean accept without deflection. None of this, "Oh that? That was nothing." Just say, "Thank you so much."

None of this, "It could have been better." Just, "Thank you so much. That means a lot to me."

If you are living for applause, you are living from a split intention—either do the thing you long to do, or try to get the audience to love you, but you can't do both and do either honestly.

Morning: Practice accepting applause today. Perhaps the applause comes in the form of a compliment: "What a lovely necklace!" Your job is to swallow your first response, which might be, "This old thing?" and to say, "Thank you so much. I love it too."

Evening: Accept, don't expect. What does this mean in your life?

December 15

"Rest is not idleness, and to lie sometimes on the grass under trees on a summer's day, listening to the murmur of the water, or watching the clouds float across the sky, is by no means a waste of time."

—JOHN LUBBOCK

I used to think napping equaled laziness and that sleep was a waste of time when I had so, so much to do. Or that it was a guilty pleasure.

I don't think that anymore.

Morning: Rest.

Evening: How can you make time for rest every day?

December 16

"What you do, the way you think, makes you beautiful."

—SCOTT WESTERFELD

There is a measurement of beauty that, in our image-obsessed world, we have forgotten.

Beauty is the way you treat others.

Beauty is the way you treat yourself.

Beauty is the measure of your kindness.

Beauty is the measure of your open-mindedness.

Beauty is the measure of your wholeheartedness.

So far beyond your skin and the way it drapes across your bones. All that leaves, but love, kindness, generosity, and open-mindedness do not fade.

Morning: Are you beautiful? What would you like to change about yourself to become more beautiful?

Evening: How can you distance yourself from constant cultural messages of physical beauty in order to appreciate your internal beauty?

December 17

*"I was the shyest human ever invented, but I had
a lion inside me that wouldn't shut up!"*

—INGRID BERGMAN

One of my favorite T-shirts has a young woman's face with her mouth wide open and "Roar" written below it. It feels like a message of empowerment, and even so, I understand fully that each of us roars in a different way—some of us may roar with our mouths closed, for instance.

My roar is not yours. And that's okay—it's not even important that I understand that your roar is a roar. It's only important that you understand it is a roar, and that you satisfy that lion inside you. Roaring is an inside job, contrary to popular belief.

Morning: Roar today. Let that lion inside you out.

Evening: What did that roar look like for you?

December 18

"Mystification is simple; clarity is the hardest thing of all."

—JULIAN BARNES

When you peel away all the extraneous bits, what is left in your life? What form do you find at the core?

We deflect that simple core in so many ways—by adding on to it, renovating it, making it more complex and therefore (we believe) more meaningful or successful.

What if stripping away were the most honest task, the one that will give us the greatest clarity about what matters and what doesn't?

Morning: What in your life can be simplified right now? Sometimes (often) this means stripping something away. What can be stripped away from your life?

Evening: What clarity do you seek in your life? How might you shed those things obfuscating that knowing?

December 19

"Do you know what a duvet is? . . . It's a blanket. Just a blanket. Now why do guys like you and me know what a duvet is? Is this essential to our survival, in the hunter-gatherer sense of the word? No. What are we then? . . . We are consumers. We're the by-products of a lifestyle obsession."

—FIGHT CLUB

The things we own end up owning us.

Yes, I know it's the holidays. And we are addicted to buying and giving. I get that. It's "expected."

What if we stopped and gave of ourselves instead? Our time, our presence, our shared experience rather than the exchange of things.

My friend Michael Scholtz and his wife stopped giving things to their kids at Christmas. Instead, they wake up on Christmas morning and open tickets to some surprise destination for a vacation together. Experiences, not things.

Morning: Why do you buy so much?

Evening: Presence, not presents. What does this mean to you?

December 20

"The most wasted of all days is one without laughter."

—E. E. CUMMINGS

If joy has a voice, it surely is laughter. Or maybe it is a silence so potent and full, it is almost bursting. Or perhaps it is the sound stars make when their light finally reaches us, a celebration beyond twinkling. Or the pop of an exuberant balloon.

Whatever the sound our joy makes, it is ours to give voice to. What happens when we share joy? It becomes infectious, the feel of it in our hearts passing on to others.

Morning: What is your voice of joy? How do you express it? Try out that voice today.

Evening: How does it feel to express joy? How does it feel to suppress it?

December 21

"I like the scientific spirit—the holding off, the being sure but not too sure, the willingness to surrender ideas when the evidence is against them: this is ultimately fine—it always keeps the way beyond open—always gives life, thought, affection, the whole man, a chance to try over again after a mistake—after a wrong guess."

—WALT WHITMAN

Don't spend your life being trained against surprise.
    Spend your life being trained *for* surprise.

Morning: Imagine your job today is to embody the scientific spirit. Be sure, but not too sure. Be willing to surrender ideas and start over.

Evening: How often do you find yourself thinking, "Don't confuse me with the facts; I have my mind made up"? Can you keep the way open instead?

December 22

"As one old gentleman put it, 'Son, I don't care if you're stark nekkid and wear a bone in your nose. If you kin fiddle, you're all right with me. It's the music we make that counts.'"

—ROBERT FULGHUM

What matters has nothing to do with how we look.

What matters most is not who you are and who I am, but the quality of the engagement between us, the music we can make.

What matters most will become very clear at the end of our lives—but the quality of our lives will be deeply changed and enhanced if we can come to this understanding before then.

Morning: Look beyond the surface today.

Evening: How can you deepen the quality of your engagement with what truly matters in the world?

December 23

*"If we have no peace, it is because we have
forgotten that we belong to each other."*

—MOTHER TERESA

I end every speech with this quote, I believe it so deeply. It is easy to see and feel that we belong to each other with people we love, isn't it? The challenge comes when we come across people with whom we can't identify—and that is where the real work is.

Every person you meet and don't meet—you belong to each other. This is where peace will be found, and only here.

It seems impossible. Start small.

Morning: Today, with every person you pass or meet, say silently to yourself, "We belong to each other." Notice what happens inside you when you say that.

Evening: What inkling toward peace did you feel today?

"Narratives are the primary way in which we make sense of our lives, as opposed to, for example, schema, cognition, beliefs, constructs. Definitions of narrative include the important element of giving meaning to events and experiences over time by connecting them as a developing, continuing story."

JACQUI STEDMON

We are story-making animals, hardwired for story. You may not realize it, but every day you are writing the story of your life. You get to choose how to give meaning to the events and experiences in your life—and you do choose, daily, whether you are conscious of doing so or not.

Imagine your life as a movie. Every movie has a trajectory of yearning—the main character wants something. And every movie has a series of obstacles the main character must "overcome" in some way. The plot of the movie is the interaction of those obstacles with that yearning, and we get to watch the character choose whether to invest in the obstacles or invest in the yearning.

Morning: In which story are you investing? The story of what you want most, or the story of why you can't get it?

Evening: What is the story of what you want?

December 25

"I would rather be able to appreciate things I cannot have than to have things I am not able to appreciate."

—ELBERT HUBBARD

Write a thank-you note today. Or two. Or more.
Appreciation is to be shared.

Morning: To whom will you write a thank-you note today?

Evening: To whom will you write a thank-you note tomorrow, and the next day?

December 26

"Every now and then a man's mind is stretched by a new idea or sensation, and never shrinks back to its former dimensions."

—OLIVER WENDELL HOLMES SR.

As with so many things, this rock has meaning on both a physical and mental plane: We have to move it or lose it. This is true of our bodies, and it is true of our minds.

Having a legacy of Alzheimer's in my family, I consciously take part in activities that require use of different parts of my brain: Reading, writing, learning the fiddle among them. Will this stave it off? I have no idea, but I will have a rich life in the meantime because of reading, writing, and learning the fiddle, so I see it as a win-win.

So, too, with our bodies. We must stretch them to stay limber and agile as we age.

Morning: How are you stretching yourself?

Evening: If you are not stretching enough, how can you change that?

December 27

"We are used to cleaning the outside house, but the most important house to clean is yourself—your own house—which we never do."

—MARINA ABRAMOVIĆ

A house with pets and kids and humans is a breeding ground for entropy and decay. In the midst of the beautiful chaos, I've adopted one simple practice: When I leave any room, I take something with me that belongs in another place. There is a glass beside my bed? When I leave the room, it goes to the kitchen. There is a box of cards on the dining room table? When I leave the room, it goes back to the front closet.

Simple, yet powerful. Never leave a room without picking up something that belongs somewhere else and taking it there. The impact is incremental, but meaningful.

So, too, with our internal houses. Things are out of place? Every day, pick something up and put it away, or give it away. Declutter your internal life.

Morning: Practice the "never leave a room without carrying something with you" rule and see what happens.

Evening: What do you need to tidy or clean in your internal "house"?

December 28

"We cannot live only for ourselves. A thousand fibers connect us with our fellow men; and among those fibers, as sympathetic threads, our actions run as causes, and they come back to us as effects."

—HERMAN MELVILLE

As this year winds down, reconnect.

Reconnect with your inner child, that little self that was full of wonder.

Reconnect with the best of your own heart.

Reconnect with your capacity to know.

Reconnect with your willingness to not know.

Reconnect to old, beautiful scars.

Reconnect with your artist self.

Reconnect with your need to let go of people who are toxic to you.

Reconnect with the voice that says "yes" inside you.

Reconnect.

Morning: What do you want to reconnect with in the coming year? Make your own list.

Evening: On the first day of each month in the new year, review your list and make sure you reconnect with the most important people and dreams on your list.

December 29

"Turn your face to the sun and the shadows fall behind you."

—HENRY WADSWORTH LONGFELLOW

We watch our shadows as we wander, the sun behind us. Elongated images of ourselves that we are always chasing, like a child chasing her shadow on the pavement, unable to connect it to herself, but seeing it outside her always just beyond her reach. She moves, and it does. She moves, and it does.

What happens if we turn to feel the sun on our face instead, that source of life? What sun can you turn to? What can you stop chasing?

Morning: Face the sun today, that brightness in your life you've been avoiding.

Evening: What are the shadows you've been chasing? What was? What you intended to be?

December 30

"Your true home is in the here and the now."

—THÍCH NHẤT HẠNH

Isn't this what mindfulness is all about? Finding your true home in the here and now?

As you look to the new year, don't leave this year too quickly. Think about what you are grateful for in this year.

And only then, think about these two questions to help you find your way home in the new year:

1. What do I want to create?
2. What do I want to let go of?

Welcome home.

Morning: What are you most grateful for in this year? Review your gratitude lists, review your calendar, review your notes from this book.

Evening: As the year ends, answer those two questions for yourself. What do I want to create in the new year? What do I want (or need) to let go of in the new year?

December 31

As we end this year together, you and I, let me leave you with a few thoughts I've had about the coming new year, in hope of sparking your own internal dialogue:

In this new year, I would rather be . . .

wise than smart . . .
kind than clever . . .
questioning than
answering . . .
at peace than striving . . .
curious than sure . . .
playing than
pontificating . . .
approached than
ignored . . .
talked "with" than
talked "at" . . .
hugged than hated . . .
stretched than shrunk . . .
loved than feared . . .
here than missing . . .

naive than cynical . . .
dreaming than
doubting . . .
shining than
smoldering . . .
healing than hurting . . .
fixing than criticizing . . .
grateful than needy . . .
focused than fractured . . .
supportive than
critical . . .
opened up than closed
down . . .
assuming abundance
rather than lack . . .

How about you?
Mindfulness is a daily practice.

Care enough about your life and yourself to show up.
Let these rocks be your daily prompt again, and again.
There is more to dive into.

Love,

Patti

ABOUT THE AUTHOR

Patti Digh is the author of eight books, including *Life Is a Verb*, *Creative Is a Verb*, and *The Geography of Loss*. She has a tattoo on her arm with these questions from Buddha: "How well did you love? How fully did you live? How deeply did you let go?" And to those core questions, she added, "Did you make a difference?" Patti lives near Asheville, North Carolina, with her much-beloved family of humans and pets. You can find Patti at PattiDigh.com and learn about her annual Life Is a Verb Camp (summer/fall camp for adults!) on courage, creativity, and community at lifeisaverbcamp.com.

JEREMY MADEA

ABOUT THE ARTIST

"Love is the answer to every question" is the life mantra of Rock Fairy, mixed media artist, and artful blogger Kim deBroin Mailhot. She happily creates in her home studio, well loved by her husband, David, and her furry babies. For more about her Rock My World rocks, her art, and creative life, visit www.queen-of-art.blogspot.com.